WORLD WAR II

.

WORLD WAR II

Six Years That Changed World History

JELLE PETERS

Odyssea Publishing

Cover photograph: Photograph by Heinrich Hoffmann, official NSDAP photographer. Heinrich Himmler, Karl Wolff, Adolf Hitler and Reinhard Heydrich in the courtyard of Prague Castle, March 16, 1939.

Published by Odyssea Publishing.
Layout by Merijn de Haen
Cover design by Teddi Black
Maps by Michael Athanson

ISBN: 978 90 825063 0 3

If you have a question about the book, want to read more from the author, or stay informed about upcoming books by the author, go to jellepeters.com. The site also features a challenging history quiz, for those who dare.

TABLE OF CONTENTS

INTRODUCTION   7

PART 1 — WW 2.0   15

The road to war and invasion of Poland   17
The fall of France   22
Battle of Britain   25
Mussolini tries to conquer Greece   27
Hitler invades Russia — Operation Barbarossa   28
The attack on Pearl Harbor   34
The Battle of Stalingrad   39
Turning points and end of the war   42
Aftermath   46

PART 2 — HOW TO KILL AN ENTIRE PEOPLE   51

Nazi ideology   52
Isolation, oppression and emigration of the German Jews   55
Pre-war Nazi plans for Jewish emigration   60
Start of the war — Einsatzgruppen and ghettos   62
Wannsee conference and the Final Solution   67
The process of extermination — and its economy   68
The figures   74

PART 3 — A BOMB   77

Crucial discoveries and the British attempt to build the bomb   79
The Manhattan Project   84
Szilárd Petition and the decision to drop the bomb   87
Hiroshima and Nagasaki figures   90
Nuclear arms race and MAD   91

WORKS CITED   95

INTRODUCTION

Fɪʀsᴛ, ᴛʜᴀɴᴋ ʏᴏᴜ ꜰᴏʀ ʙᴜʏɪɴɢ *Wᴏʀʟᴅ Wᴀʀ II: Six Years That Changed World History*. Every writer wants to be read and I am no exception. I hope you will enjoy reading it as much as I enjoyed researching and writing it.

Second, as some of you may already know, this book is part of the earlier published work, *World 2.0: A History from Enlightenment to Terrorism and Beyond*. After it was published, some people suggested I also publish portions of the book separately, as a teaser, but also because some of the chapters could stand very well on their own. I thought this was an excellent suggestion, hence this book.

Then a short note about the footnotes, particularly for those reading this book on a Kindle or other electronic device. I used in-text citations to cite sources, i.e., placing sources between parentheses in the body of the text. The (numbered) footnotes are almost exclusively used to reveal interesting details about the topic at hand. Some of them give background information about a historic character, or the setting of a particular scene. Others share later recollections of people involved at the time. Some also give more in-depth data, such as additional information on figures, for instance where I got them and/or rival figures from other sources. I also mention debates between historians about particular subjects sometimes, without going off the rail (at least not too much, I hope). The reason for highlighting this, is that while the footnotes are at the bottom of each page in the print version, they are easy to miss when reading the electronic version.

Lastly, for those of you interested in more teasers from *World 2.0: A History from Enlightenment to Terrorism and Beyond*, as well as from my upcoming book: *History That Changed the World: From Ancient Greece to 9/11*, you are very welcome to follow me on one or more of the following sources:

Amazon Author Page | Goodreads | Twitter | Jellepeters.com

About the book

With that out of the way, let me give you some additional information on what you are about to read.

Of the twenty-three chapters in *World 2.0*, three are about the events surrounding the Second World War. *WW 2.0*, *How to Kill an Entire People* and *A bomb*.

WW 2.0 discusses the events leading up to the war and how it subsequently plays out in Europe and the Pacific. It includes several major battles and campaigns, such as:

- Blitzkrieg
- Evacuation of Dunkirk
- Battle of Britain
- Operation Barbarossa
- Battle of Stalingrad
- Pearl Harbor
- Battle of Midway

How to Kill an Entire People discusses the Holocaust. Of all the topics I researched for *World 2.0*, this was the hardest. I was already well-acquainted with this dark chapter in human history, but it is one thing to know about something, quite another to have to dissect it, wade through it, keep peeling away the layers, until you are finally at a point where you are reading about how much time someone from the Sonderkommando was allotted to pull the gold teeth from sixty gassed corpses.

You will find the writing detached from these emotions though. Books and essays about the systematic destruction of the Jews, gypsies, gays and mentally insane are often accompanied by emotional adjectives, expressing the writer's horror, incomprehension and disgust. I wanted to avoid that. Emotions are for novelists.

The third and last part, *A bomb*, is about the events leading to the creation and subsequent deployment of the atomic bomb. It starts with the British, who were the first to make a serious effort to develop the bomb. They later convinced the Americans to join them, who then took the required research and production facilities to a whole different level with the so-called Manhattan Project, eventually leading to the successful Trinity Test at the Alamogordo Bombing and Gunnery Range, some 200 miles from Los Alamos, on July 16, 1945.

One of the leading scientists who had first warned President Roosevelt about the danger of the Nazis getting the bomb, Leó Szilárd, circulated a petition against using the bomb against Japan, warning it would trigger an international nuclear arms race. But the fear of having to fight a bloody, drawn-out war on mainland Japan ultimately carried more weight than the loss of tens of thousands of Japanese civilian lives and the geo-political consequences of showcasing a new bomb that could wipe entire cities off the face of the earth. Whether that was the right decision is something each of us has to answer for himself.

I hope you enjoy the book. And if you could take a minute to write a short review on Amazon and share your thoughts, I would very much appreciate it.

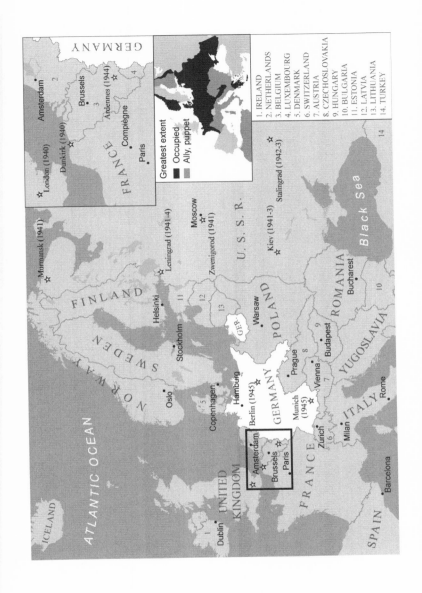

Map 1: The European Theater of the Second World War, 1939-45

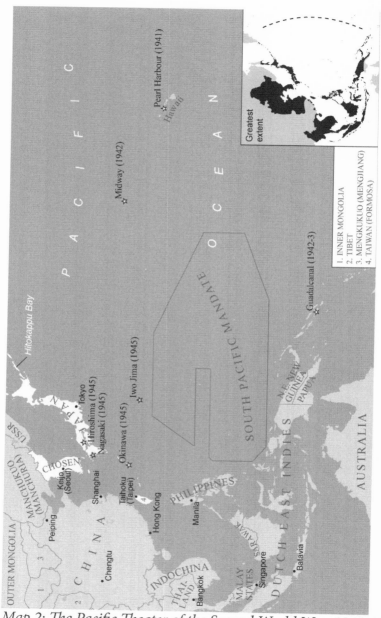

Map 2: The Pacific Theater of the Second World War, 1941-45

1

WW 2.0

"This war, like the next war, is a war to end war."[1]

David Lloyd George, British Prime Minister, 1916

"After the 'war to end war', they seem to have been pretty successful in Paris at making a 'peace to end peace.'"[2]

Brig. general Archibald Wavell,
on the results of the Paris Peace Conference, 1919

ON MAY 1, 1945, DEEP INSIDE THE *Führerbunker* underneath the Reichstag, Rochus Misch, Hitler's telephone operator and personal bodyguard, went to Joseph Goebbels and asked him if there was anything left for him to do (Schnoor, "last survivor"). Their boss had committed suicide the day before, the same day the Reichstag had been captured by the Russians. But even though the end of the Third Reich seemed a matter of hours, Misch did not just want to pick up and leave, as most of the others had done. He

---

[1]   Qtd. in Billington, 365.

[2]   Qtd. in Fromkin, "Peace", frontispiece quote.

wanted to end his service to the "*Führer, people and fatherland*" in the proper manner (qtd. in Schnoor, "last survivor"). So he went to the man whom Hitler had appointed the new Reich Chancellor in his last will and asked for instructions.

The former German Minister of Propaganda answered "*We have understood how to live, we will also understand how to die.*" (qtd. in Schnoor, "last survivor"). Later that day, Dr. Goebbels put on his hat, coat and gloves, took his wife's arm and went upstairs to the garden. There, he shot his wife, and then himself. Shortly before, Magda Goebbels had already ended the lives of their six children by crushing an ampoule of cyanide in each of their mouths (Fox, "Rochus Misch").

Misch, however, decided not to shoot himself but escape instead. He was one of the last to leave the *Führerbunker*—alive at least. As a member of the elite SS unit *Leibstandarte SS Adolf Hitler*, Misch had also been there at the beginning of the war, six years earlier, in September 1939, when Germany had invaded Poland.[3] In fact, his actions on the Polish front and the serious wound to the chest he sustained there had been one of the reasons for his promotion to the Führer's personal protection unit, the *Führerbegleitkommando* (Misch, 4).

---

3   Misch had enlisted voluntarily with the *SS-Verfügungstruppe*, a predecessor of the *Waffen-SS*, in 1937. He was called to the elite SS unit *Leibstandarte-SS Adolf Hitler* that same year (Misch, 4,19–20).

The road to war and invasion of Poland

The German invasion of Poland marked the beginning of the Second World War, as it prompted England, France and the Commonwealth nations of Canada, Australia, New-Zealand and South Africa to declare war on Germany. That declaration of war was a direct consequence of a British pledge, six months earlier, to lend Poland *"all support in their power"* in the event its independence was threatened.[4] The pledge, in turn, was a direct consequence of the German invasion of Czechoslovakia in March 1939, despite previous guarantees of German Reich Chancellor Adolf Hitler not to do so.

The reason Hitler had decided to attack Poland anyway was not because he wanted to go to war with England and France, but because he thought he wouldn't have to. And not without reason. After all, they hadn't undertaken any action after his earlier transgressions either, having opted for the political strategy of appeasement instead, i.e., trying to prevent war by giving in to most of his demands.

Since coming to power in 1933, Hitler had started a German rearmament campaign and remilitarized the Rhineland, both in violation of the Treaty of Versailles of 1919.[5] He had also annexed Austria in

---

4   Said by British Prime Minister Neville Chamberlain in a statement in the House of Commons, on March 31, 1939 (Chamberlain, "Statement").

5   Articles 42, 43 and 44 of Section III of the Versailles Treaty

March 1938 (euphemistically dubbed the '*Anschluss*') and Czechoslovakia in March 1939, the latter in clear violation of the Munich Agreement.

The Munich Agreement of September 1938 had already been a major concession from England and France to Germany, allowing it to annex a large part of Czechoslovakia known as Sudetenland, simply because it was mainly inhabited by German-speaking people who wanted to be part of Germany.

Czechoslovakia was one of the new nations that had been created after World War I from parts of the former empires of Germany, Austria-Hungary and Russia. When the Third Reich annexed German-speaking Austria in March 1938 and then hungrily eyed German-speaking Sudetenland, the British and French convinced themselves that Hitler's demand wasn't all that unreasonable.[6-7] So, at a hastily organized conference in Munich, Germany, late September that same year, England and France, eager—perhaps too eager—to keep the peace, agreed

---

forbade Germany to maintain and assemble armed forces or construct any fortifications, a violation of which was said to "*disturb the peace of the world*", according to article 44 ("Versailles Treaty"). For clauses on German armed forces, see section V of the treaty, Military, Naval and Air Clauses, articles 159–213.

6   Other European nations (re)established after WW I were Austria, Hungary, Yugoslavia, Poland, Finland, Estonia, Latvia and Lithuania.

7   The term 'Third Reich' meant to designate Nazi Germany as the third German Empire, after the Holy Roman Empire and the German Empire of 1870–1918.

to German occupation of Sudetenland, as long as the rest of Czechoslovakia would be left alone (incidentally, Czechoslovakia itself had not even been invited to the conference).

Hitler happily agreed and a relieved British Prime Minister Neville Chamberlain flew back to London, where he showed the piece of paper with Hitler's signature on it and declared it meant *"peace for our time"*.[8] Six months later Hitler invaded the rest of Czechoslovakia.

Of course it was more than a little astonishing that Germany was able to basically dictate terms to Britain and France just twenty years after losing a devastating war that had left it at the mercy of those same countries, one of which had shown particularly little leniency in imposing and enforcing harsh sanctions to ensure its neighbor to the East would never again pose a threat.

And they hadn't been exactly easy years either. The Versailles Treaty of 1919 had stripped Germany of a large part of its territory, forced it to acknowledge that it alone had been guilty of the war (*Alleinschuld*) and charged it with paying hefty reparations to the victors. When it could no longer keep up those payments a few years later, French and Belgian soldiers had

---

8   In a statement made in front of #10 Downing Street, London, on September 30, 1938 (Chamberlain, "Peace").

occupied the Ruhr, the heart of Germany's industrial area, causing its economy to collapse.[9]

In 1929, just when the German economy was getting back on its feet again thanks in part to American loans, stock markets crashed and the Great Depression started, causing U.S. investors to pull out and the economy to collapse again. Under those trying circumstances it was hardly surprising that in 1933, the fragile democracy of the newly formed German Republic (a.k.a. Weimar Republic) gave way to the totalitarian rule of Adolf Hitler and his National-Socialist Party.

Six years and a string of appeasement offerings later, Hitler gambled that he could annex Poland just as he had annexed Austria and Czechoslovakia, without any meaningful counter-action from the English or the French.

Still, mindful of the mistakes Germany had made in the Great War— a war he had fought in himself as a young corporal—Hitler took out an insurance policy against a possible two-front war, signing a secret non-aggression pact with the Soviet Union just days

---

9   Germany could pay off the reparations in cash or in kind, for instance with deliveries of coal, timber and other commodities. From the start, it frequently missed payments and goods deliveries. Some historians have argued that Germany could have paid more easily and in fact actively sabotaged an economically feasible repayment plan. (Boemeke, 402–04). In *The Treaty of Versailles: A reassessment after 75 Years*, Boemeke et al. discuss several historians who have been critical of Germany's inability to pay the WWI reparations.

before the attack on Poland. Although the fascists and communists were sworn enemies, Hitler correctly assumed that fellow dictator Joseph Stalin would be willing to strike a deal on Poland and the "*territorial and political rearrangement*" of other Eastern European countries (i.e., divvy them up between the two of them), especially with Japan biting at Russia's heels in the Far East and the Russian Army still reeling from the loss of many of its best officers during the Great Purge of 1936–39.[10]-[11]

The British and French declaration of war—while morally supportive—did nothing to save Poland from being overrun by two mighty armies in September 1939. First, German tanks and storm troopers quickly occupied the 'German half' of Poland, after which the Russians invaded the beleaguered Eastern European nation from the other side on September 17, one day after a ceasefire with Japan had gone into effect, following the battle of Khalkin Gol.[12]

---

10   The quote is from Article 1 and 2 from the secret additional protocol—not published at the time—of the Molotov-Ribbentrop Pact, signed on August 23, 1939, in Moscow (Molotov 1939). The pact was named after Soviet Foreign Minister Vyacheslav Molotov and German Foreign Minister Joachim von Ribbentrop.

11   According to declassified Soviet archives, 681,692 people were shot for "*anti-Soviet activities*" between 1937–38 alone (Pipes, 66–67). Of the Red Army's five marshals, three were killed, of its fifteen generals, thirteen did not survive the 'Great Terror' and of the nine navy admirals only one survived.

12   Fought near the Eastern border of Mongolia and Japanese-occupied Manchuria, the battle of Khalkin Gol was a decisive Russian

After Poland had been devoured, nothing much happened in Europe for six months, leading some to call this second world war a 'phoney war' (the Germans preferred the term *sitzkrieg*, as opposed to the *blitzkrieg* conquest of Poland).[13] But those who had seen it all before knew the only thing phony was the ominous calm hanging over Europe.

The fall of France

In the spring of 1940, the German war machine sprang into action again, invading Denmark and Norway in April, followed by a simultaneous attack on France, the Netherlands, Belgium and Luxembourg on May 10. That same day Neville Chamberlain resigned as British Prime Minister and was succeeded by Winston Churchill, an old war-horse who had fighting

---

and Mongolian victory that would lead Japan to concentrate its efforts of world conquest southward, towards China and the European colonies in Southeast Asia.

13   Several German generals would later declare at the Nuremberg Trials that had the French and the British attacked in the West during the German invasion of Poland, the German Army would have been powerless to stop their numerically vastly superior forces. General Alfred Jodl, for instance, said during his testimony at the Nuremberg Trials: *"we were never, either in 1938 or 1939, actually in a position to withstand a concentrated attack by these states [France, Poland and Czechoslovakia] together. And if we did not collapse already in the year 1939 that was due only to the fact that during the Polish campaign, the approximately 110 French and British divisions in the West were held completely inactive against the 23 German divisions."* (qtd. in "Trial of the Major War Criminals", Vol. 15, 350).

experience, commanding experience and decades of political and government experience.

Meanwhile, the French felt they were well-prepared for another defensive war against the Germans. After World War I they had constructed a massive, seemingly impenetrable line of defense in Northern France, the so-called Maginot Line. Stretching from Switzerland to Luxembourg, it was made up of 44 large works (*Gross ouvrages*), 58 small works (*Petits ouvrages*), 81 troop shelters —each capable of housing 250 soldiers—360 artillery, machine gun and anti-tank gun emplacements (casemates), 17 observation posts, numerous other supporting structures and extended anti-tank defenses (Allcorn, 12). But, as the saying goes, generals always prepare for the last war, something especially true for the French generals of the interwar period. Because while the French were busy pouring concrete into Northern France to prepare for another trench war, the Germans were busy pouring steel into the Ruhr to produce tanks and airplanes, preparing for a new form of highly mobile warfare that would soon earn the well-deserved moniker *blitzkrieg*.

No doubt the Maginot Line would have done a wonderful job in World War I, but sadly for the French, the Germans did not even engage them there this time around. German tanks first raced through the Ardennes forest in Southeast Belgium to cut off the Allied forces that had advanced into Belgium, subsequently pushing them towards the coast.[14] Soon, the British Expeditionary Force, the remains of the Belgian forces and three French armies (1st, 7th and 9th) were surrounded by the Germans in an area along the Northern coast of France.

To save them, the British sent every ship capable of staying afloat to the French harbor of Dunkirk. Destroyers, trawlers, yachts, personnel ships, naval motor boats, tugboats, minesweepers, almost 700 ships in total. The French, Dutch and Belgians provided an additional 168 ships, for a grand total hodge-podge collection of 861 ships (Churchill, "Their Finest Hour", 90). In nine days some 338,000 troops were thus evacuated to England, 100,000 of whom French. The successful evacuation almost felt like a victory to the British, but Churchill reminded the country that "*Wars are not won by evacuations.*"[15]

Meanwhile, the German forces pushed deep into France, outflanking the Maginot Line and arriving

---

14   This was *Fall Gelb* (Plan Yellow), a.k.a the Manstein Plan, after General Erich von Manstein, who had conceived it and convinced Hitler of adopting it during a personal meeting (May, 236–39).

15   The quote is from the legendary "*We Shall Fight on the Beaches*" speech, delivered by Winston Churchill before the House of Commons on June 4, 1940. In the same speech, Churchill voiced his aim of victory whatever the cost, speaking the famous words: "*We shall go on to the end, we shall fight in France, we shall fight on the seas and oceans, we shall fight with growing confidence and growing strength in the air, we shall defend our Island, whatever the cost may be, we shall fight on the beaches, we shall fight on the landing grounds, we shall fight in the fields and in the streets, we shall fight in the hills; we shall never surrender (..).*"

in an undefended Paris on June 14.[16] With the capital lost, the French forces at the Maginot Line isolated and the Luftwaffe reigning supreme over the French skies, Marshal Philippe Pétain—who had just succeeded Paul Reynaud as Prime Minister—asked Germany for terms.

France signed the armistice on June 22. Hitler was thrilled with the victory, which in his eyes wiped out the humiliating defeat of 1918. Eager to emphasize this, and ever mindful of the power of historic symbolism, the Führer had therefore not only arranged for the French surrender to be signed in the same railway car Germany had signed the armistice in on November 11, 1918, but even had it placed at the exact same spot in the forest of Compiègne where that signing had taken place; the railway carriage was removed from the museum especially for the occasion (LIFE, "Defeat").[17]

Battle of Britain

Two weeks later the Battle of Britain began. Knowing that an invasion of the island could not be successful without commanding the skies over the channel, Hitler had charged Hermann Göring, the commander

---

16   Paris had been declared an 'open city' on June 10 by General Maxime Weygand, meaning it would not be defended (Risser, 92).

17   The railroad car was later taken to Berlin and destroyed by the Germans in 1945 (Sciolino, "North of Paris").

of the Luftwaffe, with annihilating the British Royal Air force (RAF) first.

For months, the two air forces were locked in an all-out, deadly struggle for air superiority. Daily waves of Messerschmitt Bf 109s crossed the channel to meet and engage the RAF's Hawker Hurricanes and Supermarine Spitfires protecting the English coast. Göring also launched a bomber campaign to destroy British airfields, aircraft factories and radar stations. As the campaign intensified, the Luftwaffe attacks went increasingly further inland, at one point reaching the London perimeter airfields.

But the achilles heel of the RAF was not its lack of aircraft or airstrips, it was its lack of pilots (Richards, 190–93). In his seminal work on the history of the RAF, British historian Denis Richards wrote that the number of pilots was "*distressingly less at the beginning of September* [1940] *than at the beginning of August*", a fact that was only aggravated by the fact that the new pilots, though being "*of course, magnificent material*", did not yet have the technical competence of those they replaced (Richards, 192).

The RAF nevertheless held on, if only by the skin of its teeth. In the end, a total of 2,936 RAF pilots—596 of them foreigners from Poland, New Zealand, Canada, Czechoslovakia and Australia, among other countries—successfully held the mighty Luftwaffe at bay ("Roll of Honour"). On August 20, two days after what would become known as The Hardest Day—when the Luftwaffe had thrown everything but the kitchen sink at the RAF and was still beaten back—Churchill thanked the pilots by saying that *"Never in the field of human conflict was so much owed by so many to so few."* (Churchill, "The Few").

Saving Britain from Nazi occupation was all the more important because it allowed Britain to build up its military strength and serve as the base from where the Western Allies could launch their main assault on Nazi-occupied Europe, later in the war. For this reason, the Battle of Britain could be considered an early turning point of the war.

Mussolini tries to conquer Greece

Late October 1940, around the same time the Battle of Britain ended, Germany's ally Italy invaded Greece.[18] Italian dictator Benito Mussolini had grand dreams of establishing a New Roman Empire and conquering Greece seemed like a solid step in that direction. The ancient Romans had done it too after all, in 146 BCE.[19]

---

18   Germany and its allies are collectively known as the Axis powers. Germany's main allies were Italy and Japan, but Hungary, Romania and Bulgaria were also part of the Axis alliance.

19   146 BCE had been a particularly good year for the Roman Republic, as it achieved total and definitive victory over both the Carthaginian Empire and the Achaean League, making it the sole superpower of the Mediterranean. The cities of Carthage (located in present-day Tunisia) and Corinth (in present-day southern Greece) were both utterly destroyed, its male citizens put to the sword, its women and children sold into slavery.

Of course the Roman legions of Lucius Mummius had not needed any help from the Germans, contrary to Mussolini's forces, who were soon stopped and then pushed back by the Greeks in a counter-offensive between late 1940 early 1941. After the 'New Roman Empire' had fought itself to a stalemate, Hitler reluctantly came to Il Duce's aid, invading Greece on April 6, 1941, and forcing its surrender two and a half weeks later. Italy would pose no further threat to anyone in the war—if it ever had.[20]

Hitler invades Russia — Operation Barbarossa

With most of Western Europe under his boot, Hitler now looked to the East. On June 22, 1941, Germany invaded the Soviet Union with almost 4 million soldiers, 3,350 tanks, 2,770 aircraft and 7,200 artillery pieces, along a front of 1,080 miles/1,800 km (Glantz, ch.1).[21] The Red Army had about 4.5 million troops in

---

20   Italy had in fact conquered Abyssinia (present-day Ethiopia) in 1936, but even though most Abyssinian soldiers had been ill-trained and equipped with antiquated rifles or less—think spears and bow and arrow—and the Abyssinian air force counted only a handful of planes and even fewer pilots, it had still taken Mussolini eight months to subdue the proud nation.

21   Russian sources cited by David Glantz in chapter 1, note 3 of *Operation Barbarossa: Hitler's Invasion of Russia 1941*, give somewhat higher estimates of soldiers, tanks and combat aircraft. Oscar Pinkus gives a figure of 3.4 million German men in his work *The War Aims and Strategies of Adolf Hitler*, but since there were also about 30 divisions of Finnish and Romanian troops involved in Barbarossa, an estimate of a grand total of almost 4 million (Axis) soldiers seems fair enough (Pinkus, 188). Pinkus also mentions the German Army had

Western Russia, about 3 million of them being close enough to be deployed on the front at the beginning of the invasion (Pinkus, 188).

Operation Barbarossa, the German codename for the invasion, was the largest invasion in history and the precursor to some of the deadliest, most brutal battles ever fought, not least because both sides were commanded by ruthless dictators who had no regard whatsoever for human lives and would stop at nothing to achieve total victory.

It was also more than 'just' an invasion aimed at conquering and occupying new territory. For Hitler and the Nazi party, the drive East was part of a perceived destiny that saw Germany expand into Central and Eastern Europe, deporting and/or enslaving and/or killing the Slavic peoples living there, so as to create more *lebensraum* ('living space') for the German people. *Generalplan Ost*, the secret Nazi plan outlining German colonization of Eastern Europe, thus categorized 31 million out of the 45 million people living in occupied Poland, Lithuania, Latvia, Estonia, Russia, Belarus and Ukraine as 'racially undesirable' (Schmuhl, 348–49).

Operation Barbarossa caught the Soviet Union completely by surprise. All three prongs of the attack—Army Group North (AGN), Army Group

---

some 600,000 motor vehicles and 650,000 horses at its disposal for artillery and supplies.

Center (AGC) and Army Group South (AGS)—achieved significant advances during the early stages of the campaign. Army Group Center, for example, advanced 360 miles (600 km) in the first eighteen days of combat, inflicting more than 400,000 casualties on the Red Army, including 341,000 dead (Glantz, ch.2). The Russians also lost almost 5,000 tanks, 9,400 guns and mortars and more than 1,700 combat aircraft.

But however total the initial shock and awe of this new, audacious German blitzkrieg was, the Red Army—though seriously bleeding from several wounds—was not yet defeated, and over the course of the next month, the German advance was repeatedly bogged down by fierce Russian resistance. It became clear to the German generals they had underestimated the strength of the Soviet forces. The lengthening supply lines were also starting to become a problem, forcing the Army Groups to slow down as they waited to be resupplied.

By the end of August, only AGC had achieved its objectives, coming within 200 miles of the Kremlin and taking 800,000 prisoners in the process (Pinkus, 203). But Army Group North had so far failed to take Leningrad and link up with the Finns to the North, who in turn had yet to succeed in taking their own main objective, the port city of Murmansk. Army Group South, meanwhile, had met heavy resistance around Kiev and had not yet succeeded in taking the city, let alone advance further into southern Russia, to take control of the oil fields in the Caucasus.

In light of the situation, the generals argued that all three Army Groups should be redeployed in a single, spearheaded attack on Moscow (Pinkus, 205). Not only was the bulk of the Russian Army concentrated around the city—making an enveloping maneuver and a total, decisive victory in one battle possible— it was also a major center of arms production and an important transportation hub. And of course capturing the capital would also deal a huge blow to Russian morale, while simultaneously boosting the German one. Hitler decided against it though, because he did not want to abandon the goal of annihilating Leningrad (present-day Saint Petersburg) and linking up with the Finnish forces to the North.

On August 21, the Führer issued a directive for a dual offensive on the wings, to take Leningrad in the North and Kiev in the South (Pinkus, 224). While these operations were still underway, preparations for an offensive in the center—code named Typhoon— also began, requiring additional Infantry and Panzer divisions from both Army Group North and Army Group South, to participate in a drive for Moscow, starting on October 2 (Pinkus, 227–28).

Two weeks later, the 4th Panzer Army of General Erich Hoepner breached the Mozhaisk defense line, coming within 50 miles northeast of Moscow (Pinkus,

230). Soviet defeat seemed imminent and a matter of a few weeks at most. But then the weather joined in on the side of Mother Russia, raining (or rather, snowing) down on the infantry and turning the unpaved roads into squishy mud.

The advance was slowed down to a crawl and keeping the—already stretched—supply lines intact became next to impossible. The German High Command had no choice but to order a halt to the entire operation, so the Army Groups could reorganize and supply lines could catch up. Of course the Russians made good use of this very welcome pause, transporting troops from the Far East as fast as they could, taking the calculated (and correct) risk that the Japanese would not attack them again in the Manchurian border area (Pinkus, 234–35).[22]

Mid-November, with the roads hardened again at the onset of winter, the Germans renewed their advance, but soon after the harsh Russian winter arrived in full force, freezing tanks in the mud and soldiers in their summer uniforms. On November 21, General Heinz Guderian, commander of the Second Panzer Army, wrote in his diary: *"The icy cold, the lack of shelter, the shortage of clothing, the heavy losses of men and equipment, the wretched state of our fuel supplies, all this makes the duties of a Commander a*

---

22   Pinkus mentions the transfer of 29 infantry divisions and 9 armored brigades from the Far East to the Russian Western front, all equipped for winter warfare, unlike the German troops.

misery and the longer it goes on the more I am crushed by the enormous responsibility which I have to bear (..)" (Guderian, 251).

Late November, Hoepner's 4th Panzer Army reached Zwenigorod, about 20 miles northeast from Moscow. It was the closest the Germans would come to the Soviet capital (Pinkus, 238).

Tantalizingly close as it was, the 4th Panzer could in all honestly no longer be called a fighting force. As Hoepner wrote in a report on December 3: *"Physical and spiritual overexertion no longer endurable. In the view of the commanding generals troops no longer have any fighting capacity. The High Command is to decide about a withdrawal."* (qtd. in Pinkus, 238).[23]

On December 5 the Russians launched a counter-offensive, driving the exhausted, half-frozen German forces back some 100–200 miles (160–320 km) over a broad front (Roberts, "Stalin's Wars", 112). Unlike Napoleon Bonaparte's *Grande Armée* of 1812 though, Hitler's Wehrmacht and Waffen-SS would be back for another round in Russia, testing the resolve of the Red Army beyond all reason and rationality.

---

23   A few days later Hoepner ordered the retreat of his forces, going against Hitler's orders. A month after that he was relieved of his command. In 1944 Hoepner participated in the failed 20 July plot to assassinate Hitler. He was arrested, sentenced to death and hanged on August 8 of that same year.

The attack on Pearl Harbor

But before that second, decisive battle on the European Eastern Front, the main theater of the Second World War would first shift to the Pacific, where, on December 7, 1941, just two days after the Russians had started their counter-offensive against the Germans, the Empire of Japan launched a surprise attack on the U.S. naval base Pearl Harbor at Oahu island, Hawaii.

The attack on Pearl Harbor—home to the U.S. Pacific Fleet—was a logical decision for Japan, after negotiations with the Americans about imposed trade sanctions had faltered.

In July 1941, the United States, Great Britain and the Netherlands—whose Dutch East Indies colony (present-day Indonesia) was rich in oil—had imposed an oil embargo on Japan, in an effort to stop Japanese involvement in China and its further expansion into Southeast Asia.[24]-[25] The U.S. and Japan had subsequently opened negotiations in an effort to find a way

---

24   On July 26, 1941, President Roosevelt froze all Japanese assets in the United States by Executive Order, bringing "*all financial and import and export trade transactions in which Japanese interests are involved under the control of the Government (..)*." (qtd. in United States Government, "Peace and War", 704).

25   For several years, the U.S. had continued its oil exports to an increasingly aggressive Japan, to prevent it from attacking the Dutch East Indies for its oil supplies, which would in turn have forced the British to come to their aid, creating a war in the Pacific that would be squarely against U.S. interests. That equation changed when Japan invaded French Indochina, in September 1940, in an effort to cut off exports from there to China, with which it was already at war.

out of the rapidly deteriorating relationship, but no progress was made.

On November 20 Japan made its final offer, to withdraw its troops from southern French Indochina to northern French Indochina (to Tonkin, present-day North Vietnam), thus removing the immediate threat of an invasion of the Dutch East Indies, in exchange for U.S. cooperation with "*securing the acquisition of those goods and commodities which the two countries need in Netherlands East Indies*" (the Dutch much have loved that part), supply Japan with all the oil it required and refrain from interfering in China (qtd. in United States Government, "Peace and War", 801–02). In other words, the Empire of the Rising Sun was willing to make do with China as its sole area of expansion, as long as the oil would flow again.

On November 26, the Americans rejected this offer in the best of fashions: by way of a counterproposal that was the complete opposite of the Japanese proposal. The U.S. proposed Japan withdraw from both China and Indochina and refrain from supporting any other Chinese government than the National Government of the Republic of China (i.e., the government of Chiang Kai-shek), in exchange for the mutual unfreezing of funds and the opening of trade negotiations (United States Government, "Peace and War", 810–12).

A day earlier, Vice-Admiral Chuichi Nagumo had already left Hitokappu Bay, Japan, though, embarking on a 3,300 mile journey across the Pacific Ocean with a task force of 6 aircraft carriers, 2 battleships, 2 heavy cruisers, 1 light cruiser, 9 destroyers, 3 submarines and 8 tankers (Dull, 11).[26] He reached his destination, about 275 miles north of Oahu island, in the early hours of December 7 (Dull, 14).

At 6:00 a.m. the carriers launched the first wave of torpedo bombers, dive bombers, horizontal bombers and fighters—183 in total—which reached the U.S. Naval Station at Pearl Harbor shortly before 8:00 a.m. (Dull, 16). The two-pronged attack hit the military airfields and harbor at the same time. In the harbor, more than 90 ships—among them 8 battleships, 8 cruisers, 29 destroyers and 5 submarines—lay neatly side by side, ripe for the picking. The battleships had been designated as primary targets, along with the air bases, to prevent U.S. aircraft from repelling the attack. Shortly after the assault had begun, an armor-piercing bomb exploded in the forward ammunition magazine of the battleship USS Arizona, costing the lives of 1,177 crewmen, about half of all Americans killed during the attack (Dull, 17; Madsen,

26   Hitokappu Bay (present-day Kasatka Bay) is located on the eastern shore of Iturup, the largest of the Kuril Islands, northeast of Japan. Soviet forces occupied the Kurils in 1945. The islands are still controlled by Russia today.

173). Three other battleships were also sunk, the other four were damaged but stayed afloat.

A second wave of 167 planes was sent in at 7:15 a.m., with the same objectives as the first wave (Dull, 18). Around 10:00 a.m. all Japanese planes returned to their carriers, and less than four hours later the Imperial fleet was on its way home again. In all, 21 U.S. ships had been either sunk or damaged, 188 aircraft had been destroyed, an additional 159 aircraft had been damaged, 2,403 U.S. servicemen had been killed, and 1,178 wounded (Dull, 19).

It was bad, but it could have been even worse. A planned third wave, directed against important onshore harbor facilities—fuel depots, navy repair yards and submarine docks—was canceled by Nagumo, who feared another run might expose his fleet to an attack by the Pacific Fleet's carriers, whose whereabouts were still unknown (Dull, 19–20). Admiral Chester Nimitz, who took command of the Pacific Fleet shortly after the attack on Pearl Harbor, later said the war would have been prolonged by two years had the Japanese succeeded in destroying the fuel depots, as they carried the oil supplies for the entire fleet (Miller, 16–17).

The fact that the three aircraft carriers of the Pacific Fleet, *Enterprise*, *Saratoga* and *Lexington*, had not been at Pearl Harbor at the time, meant the U.S. could still get into the war in the Pacific fairly quickly. Had they been destroyed, the Pacific Fleet would have likely been unable to conduct any large-scale offensive operations for more than a year. The damage to the Pacific Fleet's battleships was extensive, yes, but it would be aircraft carriers and submarines, not the relatively slow battleships, that would prove to be of vital importance in the war in the Pacific.

Of course the attack instantly silenced the non-interventionists in the United States, who had previously made the case for staying out of the war. Following President Roosevelt's famous 'Infamy Speech', on December 8, Congress needed just 33 minutes to declare War on Japan, with only one Representative, the pacifist Jeannette Rankin, voting against the declaration.[27]

Three days later, Germany and Italy, honoring the Tripartite Pact with Japan, declared war on the United States. The U.S. responded in kind. The British also declared war on Japan, but Russia decided to keep its neutrality pact with Japan in place, careful not to get drawn into a two-front war with Japan attacking from the East.[28]

---

27   The 'Infamy Speech'—Roosevelt's Address to Congress of December 8, 1941—contained the famous words: "*December 7, 1941—a date which will live in infamy—the United States of America was suddenly and deliberately attacked by naval and air forces of the empire of Japan.*" Jeanette Rankin's no vote was met with "*boos and hisses*", according to an article in the New York Times at the time (Kluckhohn, "U.S. Declares War"; Roosevelt, "Day of Infamy").

28   The Soviet-Japanese Neutrality Pact had been signed on April

The Battle of Stalingrad

It was a smart move on Stalin's part, because in the summer of 1942 Germany launched a second massive offensive on Soviet territory, code-named *Fall Blau* (Case Blue). The primary objective was to capture the Caucasus oil fields in the South, the main Russian source of oil (Fritz, 231–32). To protect the left flank of the advance into the Caucasus, the city of Stalingrad (present-day Volgograd) had to be captured as well— or at least neutralized. It was also where Stalin decided to make his last stand.

One month into the German offensive, Stalin issued the (in)famous Order No. 227, a.k.a. the 'Not one step back' order. Signed by "*the national commissar for defense: J. Stalin*", the order was not meant to simply boost morale or instill fear of insubordination in the troops, but sought to actually root out all unauthorized retreats, whatever the circumstances, using harsh but effective measures (Stalin, Order 227). Officers that allowed unauthorized retreats would be unconditionally removed from command and sent to court martial. Each army was also to set up 'penal companies', where those "*guilty of a breach of discipline due to cowardice or bewilderment will be sent, and put...on more difficult sectors of the front to give them an opportunity to redeem by blood their crimes against the Motherland*"

13, 1941, just two months before Germany launched Operation Barbarossa against the Soviet Union. The pact would remain in place until April 5, 1945, when the Soviet Union denounced it.

(Stalin, Order 227). Furthermore, 'defensive squads' would be placed behind 'unstable divisions', to "*shoot in place panic-mongers and cowards and thus help the honest soldiers of the division execute their duty to the Motherland*".

With one army thus determined to conquer at all cost and the other to defend at all cost, the epic struggle for Stalingrad began.

Between August 23, 1942-February 2, 1943, the unfortunate city was reduced to little more than a vast field of ruins, a cemetery for the hundreds of thousands—if not more than a million—of soldiers and civilians that perished there.[29]

Mid-November 1942, the Germans were tantalizingly close to victory, holding more than 90 percent of the city, but when winter set in they still had not broken the back of the 62nd Army, which, charged with holding Stalingrad at all cost and commanded by General Vasily Chuikov, had been able to entrench itself in a 16-mile strip in the city, alongside the Volga's west bank (Roberts, "Victory at Stalingrad", 85).

Chuikov developed several urban war tactics during the battle for Stalingrad, such as instructing

---

29   In *Enemy at the Gates: The Battle for Stalingrad*, William Craig estimates the total casualties for both sides at 1,520,000, of which 750,000 Soviet soldiers, 400,000 Germans, 130,000 Italians, 120,000 Romanians and 120,000 Hungarians (Craig, xiv). Richard Overy mentions 500,000 Russian and 147,000 German dead in *Russia's War: A History of the Soviet War Effort: 1941–1945*, (Overy, 185). The total number of civilian casualties remains unknown.

his commanders to fight with small groups wielding machine guns, grenades and Molotov Cocktails, instead of committing whole companies and battalions at a time (Chuikov, 150). He also found a way to decrease the effectiveness of the German Luftwaffe, by reducing *"the no-man's land as much as possible - to the throw of a grenade"*, making it much harder for the Luftwaffe to bomb Soviet frontline positions (Chuikov, 84). As Chuikov later wrote: *"City fighting is a special kind of fighting. Things are settled here not by strength, but by skill, resourcefulness and swiftness."* (Chuikov, 146).

Two other fundamental problems for the Germans were logistics and the lack of reserves. Equipment, fuel, food, ammunition, medicine, it was all much harder to come by for the Germans, who were fighting far away from home, than for the Russians, who were fighting for their home. At several critical moments of the months-long battle, General Chuikov's forces were replenished by the timely arrival of reinforcements, while those of his main adversary, General Friedrich Paulus, Commander of the German 6th Army, were not (Roberts, "Victory at Stalingrad", 90–91).

When, late November, the 6th Army was encircled during a Russian counter-offensive, Paulus requested permission to try and break out, but Hitler refused, ordering him to hold his position (Jukes, 107–08). Paulus complied, but two months later—the situation of his army by then utterly desperate and destitute—he sent another message to Hitler, asking for the permission to surrender. The Führer refused again, shooting back: "*Surrender is out of the question. The troops will defend themselves to the last*." (qtd. in Roberts, "Victory at Stalingrad", 132).

On January 31, 1943, the 6th Army nevertheless surrendered, although Paulus left the actual surrendering to someone else and also refused to sign or issue orders for his men to surrender (Roberts, "Victory at Stalingrad", 133). Two days later, On February 2, the remaining German forces in Stalingrad also surrendered.

One of the deadliest battles in history, Stalingrad would prove to be the turning point of the war in Europe. Germany never really regained the initiative on the Eastern front after it, but instead began its long retreat back to the *Heimat*.[30]

Turning points and end of the war

In September 1943, a couple of months after the British had defeated the Axis forces in North Africa, the Western Allies invaded the Italian mainland. With

---

30   The Germans did mount another offensive in July 1943, code-named *Unternehmen Zitadelle* (Operation Citadel), but it was successfully countered by the Red Army before achieving any significant breakthrough. The failure of *Zitadelle* was at least partly caused by British intelligence on German preparations for the offensive finding its way to Stalin—both officially and unofficially, as the Soviets had a spy inside the British code-breaking center at Bletchley Park—two months before it was launched (Copeland, 4–6).

the subsequent Allied invasion in Normandy less than a year later, on June 6, 1944 (D-Day), the Western Allies delivered on their promise to Stalin to open up a second front, though the Soviet dictator never stopped believing the Americans and British had deliberately delayed their invasion to let the Soviet Union suffer the brunt of the German onslaught.

The turning point of the War in the Pacific, meanwhile, came a few months before Stalingrad, at the Battle of Midway (June 4–7, 1942), when the Japanese Navy lost four aircraft carriers while sinking only one U.S. carrier. It also lost some 270 aircraft and—much worse—125 experienced pilots, more than half of the Japanese pilots who had entered the battle (Isom, 229–36).[31] The defeat seriously crippled the offensive capabilities of the Japanese fleet and increasingly forced it on the defensive.

Following the emboldening victory at Midway, the Allies decided to invade the Japanese-occupied island of Guadalcanal (part of the present-day Solomon Islands), east of New Guinea. The main reason for the attack was to prevent the Japanese Navy from using the island as a base from where supply routes between Australia and the U.S. could be threatened.

---

31   Dallas Isom writes in *Midway Inquest* that the loss of the experienced pilots hurt the Japanese Navy more than that of the four carriers; the pilots were never replaced and the remaining attack carriers could no longer be provided with a full contingent of first-line pilots (Isom, 236).

In February 1943, after six months of heavy fighting, the Japanese finally surrendered the island to the Allied forces. Over the next two years, several other Japanese-held islands would follow in similar fashion, as the Americans slowly but certainly advanced towards mainland Japan by way of their *island-hopping* strategy.

Back in Europe, no hopping was necessary to advance towards Germany. After a last failed German offensive in the Ardennes (December 16, 1944-January 25, 1945) Western Allied forces crossed the Rhine in March 1945 and fanned out across Germany. By then the Red Army had already advanced into Germany from the East, and on April 25 American and Russian forces linked up at the Elbe river. Five days later Hitler committed suicide in his bunker and two days after that Berlin fell. On May 8, shortly before midnight, the German Supreme Command of the Armed Forces surrendered unconditionally in Berlin. [32]

After the defeat of Germany, the U.S. started preparations for their invasion of the Japanese mainland

---

32 The German Instrument of Surrender had actually already been signed in Reims, on May 7, but the Soviet Union had formally protested that the signed document was not the same as the draft that had been prepared earlier and that the Soviet Representative in Reims, General Susloparov, had not been been authorized to sign the document of surrender. The Soviets also considered Berlin a far more suitable location for the ceremonial surrender of Nazi Germany than Reims, hence the second, official surrender in Berlin on May 8 (Pinkus, 501–03).

(code-named *Operation Downfall*). Given their experience against the Japanese Army in several brutal island battles such as Guadalcanal, Iwo Jima and Okinawa, estimates about American casualties in the event of an invasion of Japan ranged from approximately 200,000 to as high as 4 million.[33] Staggering figures that are still used as the principal justification for the subsequent atomic bombings of the Japanese cities of Hiroshima and Nagasaki on August 6 and 9, 1945, respectively, meant to compel Japan to surrender without having to invade it first. The two bombs likely killed upwards of 250,000 people (Holdstock, 2). Six days later Japan surrendered unconditionally.[34]

The war was over, but the world would never be the same.[35]

---

33   Of course nobody could predict casualty rates with any certainty. All estimates looked at previous campaigns and tried to account for the likely level of participation from the Japanese civilian population. Thus, General Curtis LeMay arrived at 500,000 casualties, while a study by the Joint Chiefs of Staff estimated around 456,000 casualties—including 109,000 dead or missing—for the first part of the campaign, climbing to a total of 1,200,000 casualties of which 267,000 fatalities for the second part. Another study, done for the Secretary of War, estimated that conquering Japan in its entirety in case of large-scale participation by civilians could cost as much as 1.7–4 million American casualties.

34   The formal signing of the Japanese Instrument of Surrender took place in Tokyo Bay, aboard the USS Missouri, on September 2, 1945.

35   World War II casualty estimates mostly range between 40–75 million, but as Matthew White points out in his excellent work about the 100 deadliest episodes in human history, a majority of

Aftermath

The center of geopolitical power had shifted from Europe to the United States and the Soviet Union, two countries that would soon find themselves on opposing sides in everything except for a shared, basic understanding that mankind might not survive another world war.

In the decades that followed, the world would be largely divided into an American/Western/capitalist sphere of influence and a Russian/Eastern/communist sphere of influence. So too in Europe, with democracy restored and far-reaching economic and military cooperation established between Western Europe and the U.S., while Eastern Europe, liberated by the Red Army, would remain under Soviet influence, frequently enforced heavy-handedly.

And then there was the Bomb. For a few years, the U.S. remained the only country that had it, but on August 29, 1949, the U.S.S.R successfully tested an atomic weapon of its own, thus ushering in the era of Mutually Assured Destruction (MAD). Fortunately for all of us, despite a dark dalliance with nuclear war in 1962, the East-West conflict would largely remain a 'Cold War', although several

---

historians—among them John Haywood, John Keegan, Charles Messenger and J.M Roberts—arrive at a total of 50 million military and civilian deaths (White, 605). The likely high number of civilian deaths combined with the general lack of reliable population data is the reason there is so much variation between the different estimates.

proxy wars were fought—in Greece, China, Korea, Vietnam, Afghanistan, to name a few—to keep things interesting.[36]

WW II also spelled the end for the European colonial empires, with decolonization waves rolling through Africa, Asia and the Middle East in the 1940s, 1950s and 1960s. They would bring independence, but also instability and in many cases (civil) war.

Another independent nation owing its existence to the Second World War finally gave the Jews a home of their own again, but the creation of the state of Israel, in 1948, would come at the cost of great instability in the Middle East, which lasts to this day.

Still, after all the carnage, cruelty and destruction there was also hope, in the form of a burgeoning understanding that all human life is precious and that war should no longer be accepted as a means to an end in a modern world. On this shared conviction—however fragile, imperfect and at times ambiguous—the United Nations and the Universal Declaration of Human Rights were created.

Rochus Misch, one of the last to leave the *Führerbunker* alive on May 2, 1945, was captured by the Russians shortly after his escape. He spent the next nine years as a Soviet prisoner, before returning to Berlin in 1953, where he lived out the remainder

---

36   For the 1962 Cuban Missile Crisis, see *The Cuban Missile Crisis: How Close We Really Came to Nuclear War*.

of his life just two miles from the location of Hitler's last hideout (Schnoor, "last survivor"). The last survivor of the *Führerbunker*, Misch died on September 5, 2013. He remained loyal to his Führer until the end.

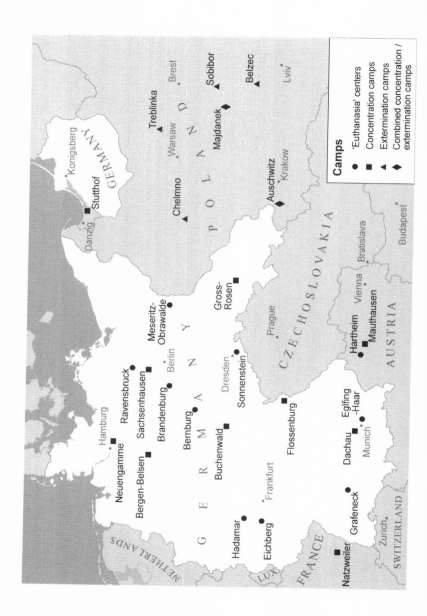

Map 3: Nazi Camps, 1933-45

2

HOW TO KILL AN ENTIRE PEOPLE

"Technically? That wasn't so hard—it would not have been hard to exterminate even greater numbers (..) The killing itself took the least time. You could dispose of 2,000 head in a half hour, but it was the burning that took all the time. The killing was easy; you didn't even need guards to drive them into the chambers; they just went in expecting to take showers and, instead of water, we turned on poison gas. The whole thing went very quickly."[1]

Rudolf Höss, Commandant of Auschwitz, 1946

IN 2008, SEVENTEEN-YEAR-OLD ELI SAGIR GOT A tattoo after returning from a high school trip to Poland. Nothing too elaborate or complicated, just a number. 157622 (Rudoren, "Proudly Bearing"). When she showed it to her grandfather, he bent his head and kissed it, because he had the same number, in the same spot. Only he hadn't gotten his at a hip tattoo parlor but at Auschwitz concentration camp, nearly 70 years ago.

---

1   Qtd. in Gilbert, 249–50.

Several other young descendants of Auschwitz survivors have done the same. They view the number as part of their family history, an heirloom almost. They want to remember. They want others to remember. Not surprisingly, the young, numbered forearms trigger reactions far and wide. Some are disgusted, shocked, even angry. Others find it a beautiful gesture (Rudoren, "Proudly Bearing").

It is not all that different from how Auschwitz survivors treated their own tattoo. Some rushed to the plastic surgeon after the war to have the numbers removed, others viewed it as a scar that nevertheless needed to be preserved. Still others viewed it with pride, because it proved they survived. Everything.

Nazi ideology

For some of the few that remain, surviving started almost immediately after the *Nationalsozialistische Deutsche Arbeiterpartei* (NSDAP, a.k.a the Nazi Party) came to power in Germany, in 1933. NSDAP leader Adolf Hitler had never made a secret of his hatred for the Jewish people (or many other people for that matter), a hatred emphatically shared by the Nazi Party electorate and even by many who had not voted for the Nazis in 1933.[2] In fact, Jews had been subject

---

2   In his autobiographical manifesto *Mein Kampf* (My Struggle) Hitler writes: "*If one considers how much he has sinned against the masses in the course of the centuries, how again and again he squeezed and extorted without mercy, if one considers further how the people gradually learned to hate him for this and finally saw in his existence*

to hatred, discrimination and violence for centuries throughout Europe. They were used to it. But this time, in this country, it would be different.

The Nazi ideology was centered around the belief in the superiority of the Aryan race, the German *Volk* (people) and German culture. To fulfill its perceived destiny of world domination, Germany needed to have a strong state, a strong leader and a strong people. The state should therefore be given the means to control and legislate every aspect of society and its citizens, and the leader should be given the means to control every aspect of the state—the so-called *Führerprinzip* (Bendersky, 41–42).[3] The people, for their part, should be pure of blood and purpose, willing to sacrifice everything for the good of the state.

Everybody who disagreed with this view was to be considered a disruptive force to the strength of the state and therefore a danger to the security of the state. Everybody who was impure of blood or weak in any other way could not be part of the New Order and should either be reeducated (if only weak) or permanently expelled (if impure).[4] These *Unerwünschten*

---

really nothing but a punishment of Heaven, then one can understand how hard this change must be for the Jew." (Hitler, 431). And: *"Therefore, I believe today that I am acting in the sense of the Almighty Creator: By warding off the Jews I am fighting for the Lord's work."* (Hitler, 84).

3   In chapter three of *A History of Nazi Germany: 1919–1945*, Bendersky also discusses the historical roots of Nazi ideology.

4   That the National Socialists meant business regarding the 'purification' of the German *Volksgemeinschaft* became clear just a couple

(undesirables) included Jews, Slavs, Gypsies, blacks, communists, homosexuals, the mentally ill, the disabled, Jehovah's Witnesses and Freemasons.

But above all, the Jews.

Still, although getting rid of the Jews stood front and center of the Nazi ideology, actually getting it done posed various practical challenges. It is one thing to shout all manner of things in speeches at beer cellars and backrooms, but quite another to turn those rants into actual policy. An estimated 530,000 Jews lived in Germany alone in 1933 (Nicosia, 4). They served in the military, taught at universities, sat on judge's benches, worked as doctors, lawyers, in factories, owned shops, stocks, bonds, houses, employed people, married, had children. Whatever their perceived undesirability, their lives were entwined with all aspects of German society.

Historians still debate whether Hitler had already decided to exterminate all the Jews even before he came to power, but given the different solutions to the 'Jewish Question' the Nazis tried out between 1933–41

---

of months after they came to power, when Wilhelm Frick, the newly appointed Reich Minister of the Interior, implemented the 'Law for the Prevention of Genetically Diseased Offspring' (*Gesetz zur Verhütung erbkranken Nachwuchses*), in July 1933. This law provided the state with the power to forcibly sterilize those suffering from a hereditary disease. Around 400,000 people would subsequently be sterilized over the next decade and thus in many cases be permanently expelled from the gene pool (Crew 113–14).

it seems unlikely he had, even if only for practical reasons. After all, the Germany of 1933 was very different from that of 1941. For one thing, Germany was not at war with anybody in 1933, nor was it ready for war. Its armed forces were relatively small compared to countries like France and Great Britain. What would these countries have done if the Nazis had started exterminating the Jews then and there? And what would the German people have done if their Jewish officers, teachers, professors and colleagues had been dragged away in the middle of the night? In hindsight, the answer to both questions is: probably nothing. But in 1933, this seemed far from certain.

Isolation, oppression and emigration of the German Jews

Hitler therefore initially opted for a strategy of isolation and emigration. By isolating the Jews, their entanglement with German society would diminish, making it easier to remove them altogether later on. It would also create jobs for *Volksgenossen* (compatriots; only Germans of pure blood could be a *Volksgenosse*), an advantage not to be discarded in times of economic depression.[5]

---

5   Point 4 of the National Socialist Program stated: "*Only those who are our fellow countrymen can become citizens. Only those who have German blood, regardless of creed, can be our countrymen. Hence no Jew can be a countryman.*" ("Program").

The first major law aimed directly at pushing Jewish German citizens out of society was the *Law for the Restoration of the Professional Service*. It was adopted on April 7, 1933, just two weeks after the Reichstag had passed the *Enabling Act*, which gave Hitler dictatorial powers.[6] The law excluded all those of non-Aryan descent—as well as opponents of the Nazi regime—from working as civil servants. It meant Jews could no longer serve as teachers, judges or professors. Not long after that, a similar law was passed forbidding Jews to work as lawyers, doctors, notaries or tax consultants, while another restricted the number of Jewish students at schools and universities, later excluding them from educational institutions altogether.

In enforcing these laws, however, a new problem surfaced. One that hadn't been given much consideration before, perhaps because it didn't make for very sexy anti-Semitic election rhetoric. Now that anti-Semitic rhetoric had become government policy though, it needed to be addressed. The problem lay

---

6   The Enabling Act of 1933 gave the cabinet the right to enact laws without the consent of the Reichstag (by passing this law the Reichstag thus made itself superfluous). To get the necessary majority, the government had arrested all the Communist (KPD) Reichstag members and several Social Democrat (SPD) Reichstag members under cover of the Reichstag Fire Decree, a law that suspended several constitutionally guaranteed rights 'until further notice', following the alleged arson of the Reichstag by communists. With the KPD and several SPD members gone and the Center Party bullied into voting for the measure with the Nazi Party, the enabling act was passed 444 in favor, 94 against.

in determining who exactly counted as a Jew. Was it everybody who had a Jewish ancestor? But how far back? And was one enough or should there be multiple Jewish ancestors? And what if none of the Jewish ancestors were female? After all, according to the Jewish faith, only those born from a Jewish woman are considered Jewish by birth. And what about converts? Since one could become Jewish by conversion, should that mean one could also stop being Jewish, for instance by converting to Christianity?

The need to answer these questions became especially acute when, in September 1935, the Reich Ministry of the Interior wanted to introduce new laws to further isolate the Jews from German society. These Nuremberg Laws—so named because they were introduced at the annual Nazi Party rally in Nuremberg—stripped Jews of their citizenship and forbade marriage and sexual relations between Jews and Germans.[7]

After much debate, it was determined that a person who had at least three Jewish grandparents was to be considered *Volljude* (a full Jew), regardless of religious affiliation (Steinweis, "Studying the Jew", 42). A person who had two Jewish grandparents was considered a *Mischling* (crossbreed) in the first degree.

---

7   The Nuremberg Laws adopted at the Nazi Party rally were the 'Reich Citizenship Law' and the 'Law for the Protection of German Blood and German Honor' (Steinweis, "Law in Nazi Germany", 47–48).

With one Jewish grandparent one was considered a *Mischling* in the second degree. However, there were certain circumstances that could render a *Mischling* legally Jewish, making such a person a so-called *Geltungsjude*. Being a member of a Jewish congregation for instance, or being married to a Jew.

Having settled the legal definition of Jewishness, existing anti-Jewish legislation could now also be better enforced. Following the Nuremberg Laws, a host of national and local new anti-Jewish legislation was introduced, isolating the Jews ever further.

Under these circumstances it was hardly surprising that many Jews wanted to quit Germany altogether. Between 1933–38, 140,000 Jews thus emigrated from Germany, for the most part to neighboring countries like Denmark, the Netherlands, Belgium and France, countries that would unfortunately prove to be only a temporary safe haven from Nazi persecution (Nicosia, 7).[8]

After the first wave of Jewish emigration in 1933, when 37,000 left, the numbers declined again—to 23,000 in 1934 and 21,000 in 1935—partly because the situation in Germany stabilized somewhat, but

---

8   Anne Frank was one of them. Having emigrated from Germany to the Netherlands early 1934, the Frank family went into hiding after Germany invaded and occupied Holland. In August 1944 they were nevertheless arrested by the *Sicherheitsdienst* and put on transport. Anne and her sister Margot died in concentration camp Bergen-Belsen in March 1945, a few weeks before the camp was liberated by the British.

also because most countries did not want them (Longerich, 67). It prompted Zionist leader (and later first President of Israel) Chaim Weizmann to lament: *"The world seemed to be divided into two parts - those places where the Jews could not live, and those where they could not enter."* (qtd. in Sherman, 112).

To find a solution for the increasing number of Jewish refugees from Nazi Germany, an international conference was organized in Evian-Les-Bains, France, in July 1938. A few months earlier, at a speech in Königsberg, Hitler had already made it clear he would welcome any initiative in this direction, saying: *"I can only hope and expect that the other world, which has such deep sympathy for these criminals, will at least be generous enough to convert this sympathy into practical aid. We, on our part, are ready to put all these criminals at the disposal of these countries, for all I care, even on luxury ships"* (qtd. in New York Times, "Hitler").[9] 32 countries attended the conference, but the Netherlands and Denmark were the only European countries willing to accept a limited increase in the number of refugees (Landau, 138).

A couple of months later, in the night of November 9–10, 1938, thousands of Jewish homes, hospitals, schools, synagogues and businesses were destroyed, 20,000 Jews were arrested—most of whom were sent

---

9   Distasteful as the comment is, it also clearly shows Hitler was not yet committed to the destruction of the Jewish race.

to concentration camps, of which there were six at the time, mainly meant for political dissidents—and 91 people were killed (Sherman, 166–67).

Kristallnacht, so called because of the large number of shattered windows, brought Jewish persecution in Germany to a whole new level. Whoever had still been fooling himself thinking Jews might have some kind of future in Nazi Germany, could do so no longer. By June 1939, 309,000 German, Austrian and Czech Jews had applied for the 27,000 places available in the U.S. quota. By the time the war broke out, in September 1939, some 95,000 had managed to emigrate to the United States, 60,000 had emigrated to Palestine, 40,000 to Great Britain and about 75,000 to Central and South America ("German Jewish Refugees").[10]

Pre-war Nazi plans for Jewish emigration

Apart from terrorizing the Jews to stimulate emigration, the Nazis also floated several state sanctioned 'total emigration' plans. There was the *Schacht plan*—named after Hjalmar Schacht, President of the Reichsbank, who conceived it—which called for World Jewry to establish a fund that would finance the resettlement of a total of 150,000 able-bodied German and Austrian Jews, who would later be joined by 250,000 dependents (Yahil, 117). Another fund

---

10   This was out of a total of 282,000 Jews (from the initial 530,000 in 1933) that made it out of Germany between 1933–39 and 117,000 Jews that emigrated from annexed Austria ("German Jewish Refugees").

was to be established out of the emigrants' property and used to pay for maintaining those Jews who were unable to emigrate. Progress was made in subsequent negotiations with the United States and Britain, but before a version of the plan could be implemented the war broke out (Yahil, 118).

Another idea was the *Nisko Plan*, concocted in September 1939 and meant as a Jewish Reservation of sorts in occupied Poland. It resulted in the first deportations East, but a host of practical problems and bad international press as to the treatment of the deportees—at a time foreign public opinion still mattered somewhat to the Nazis—caused the plan to be shelved (Yahil, 138–40, 160–61).

The *Madagascar Plan*, which (re)surfaced in the summer of 1940, after the defeat of France, envisioned shipping the entire German Jewish population to the island of Madagascar, a French colony (Yahil, 253–54).[11] It was seriously considered by Hitler, but abandoned after Germany lost the Battle of Britain. One plan that did come to fruition was the *Transfer* (a.k.a. Haavara) *Agreement*, which facilitated the emigration

---

11   The idea to resettle European Jews on Madagascar was not a German one, the French and the Poles had also considered it in the late 1930s (Yahil, 254; Browning, 81–82). The Poles had even sent a small investigating team to the island, with consent of the French, as part of a feasibility study (Browning, 81–82). It concluded that a maximum of 5,000–7,000 families could be settled there.

of around 51,000 German Jews to Palestine between 1933–39 (Yahil, 100–04).[12]

The outbreak of the war made emigration of the remaining Jews practically impossible. Not only did it make foreign countries even less susceptible to accepting Jewish refugees, German conquests also dramatically increased the number of Jews living in the Third Reich.[13] And the fact that almost half of the German Jewish population was still living in Germany even after having been subjugated to the harshest anti-Semitic laws, made it clear that wartime emigration of three million Polish Jews just wasn't going to happen. It was time for a different answer to the 'Jewish Question'.

Start of the war — Einsatzgruppen and ghettos

On September 21, 1939, SS-*Gruppenführer* Reinhard Heydrich—whom Hitler called The Man with the Iron Heart—sent a memo to the chiefs of all the *Einsatzgruppen* of the *Sicherheitspolizei* (Security Police), concerning the "*Judenfrage im besetzten Gebiete*", the Jewish Question in Occupied Territory

---

12   Under the agreement, Jewish emigrants to Palestine had to pay 1,000 pounds sterling into a trust company in Germany, which used the funds to buy German goods and sell them to the Haavara company, which in turn sold them in Palestine, thus stimulating German export ("Encyclopedia Judaica: Haavara"). The proceeds went to the emigrants living in Palestine.

13   Poland alone, invaded in September 1939, was home to an estimated three million Jews (Yahil, 187).

(Arad, "Documents", 173–78).[14] The *Einsatzgruppen*, formed in the summer of 1939, leading up to the invasion of Poland, were SS death squads, operating in the wake of the regular army with instructions to eliminate "*all anti-German elements in hostile country behind the troops in combat.*" (Browning, 16).[15]

In the memo, Heydrich instructed the chiefs to start rounding up the Jews and put them in "*concentration centers*" (Arad, "Documents", 173–78). These ghettos, he wrote, should be located near a railroad junction or at least on a railway, to accommodate transportation of the Jews at a later date.

Jewish enterprises, factories, farms and land were to be "*aryanized*" (i.e., confiscated), though Heydrich pointed out that a transition period might be necessary in some cases, so as not to hurt German economic interests (Arad, "Documents", 173–78). The memo also talked about how "*the final aim*" (*Endziel*) of

---

14   Source includes the complete memo.

15   The *Einsatzgruppen* were controlled by the powerful *SS-Reichssicherheitshauptamt*, the Reich Main Security Office, which had been created on September 27, 1939, to bring the *Sicherheitspolizei* and the *Sicherheitsdienst* under the same roof. It was run by Heydrich. The *Einsatzgruppen* were responsible for numerous mass shootings between 1941–45, killing an estimated two million civilians, including 1.3 million Jews (Headland, 98–106). In *Messages of Murder*, Headland includes detailed killing statistics from the various *Einsatzgruppen*, before concurring with Raul Hilberg's oft-cited estimate from *The Destruction of the European Jews* that 1,300,000 Jews were killed in the East by the *Einsatzgruppen*, other SS agencies and collaborators (Headland, 106).

the measures *"will require extended periods of time"*, and that all the *"planned total measures are to be kept strictly secret"*. It therefore seems that, by September 1939, at the very least Reinhard Heydrich had made up his mind as to the faith of the Jewish population in the Reich.

Between October 1939-July 1942, more than 1,100 Jewish ghettos were created in Nazi-occupied Eastern Europe (Michman, 8). The allotted space for the ghettos was far too small for the number of Jews forced to live there. The resulting overcrowding, as well as the absence of even the most basic sanitation services, caused diseases like typhus, dysentery and diphtheria to spread fast and freely (Friedman, 122). Malnutrition was another serious problem. It was intentionally caused, by keeping food deliveries far below even the bare minimum. In the Warsaw ghetto, for instance, Jews were forced to subsist on 180 calories per day—a quarter of what was given to Poles—while also being forbidden, on pain of death, to leave the ghetto and trade for food and other essentials (Friedman, 122). Hundreds of thousands thus died of starvation, exhaustion and disease before the ghettos were liquidated in 1942–43.

The number of forced labor camps also rapidly expanded after the outbreak of the war, eventually numbering more than 30,000 including subcamps, most of them in Germany and Poland.[16] Jews, Slavs, Russian prisoners of war, Gypsies, gays and political dissidents, millions were forced to work in the camps, providing ultra cheap labor for the German industry. To sustain this economic system it needed to be fed with a continuous stream of new workers, as most prisoners succumbed within a few months to the grueling conditions. At concentration camp Buchenwald, for example, the average life expectancy of a prisoner working in the factories was nine months (Fleischman, 71).[17]

Following the German invasion of Russia (Operation Barbarossa) in June 1941, Heydrich's

---

16   Research by Geoffrey P. Megargee et al. about the full extent of Nazi camps has concluded that, contrary to what was previously believed, the total number of camps between 1933–45 was 42,500, of which 30,000 slave labor camps (including subcamps), 1,150 Jewish ghettos, 1,000 prisoner-of-war camps and 980 concentration camps. Dr. Megargee is the lead researcher of a team working on a multivolume encyclopedia that aims to document all the camps. As of 2014, the first two of an expected total of seven volumes of the *Encyclopedia of Camps and Ghettos, 1933–1945*, have been published (Lichtblau 2013).

17   According to an income statement from Buchenwald, total net revenue for a prisoner was 1,631 Reichsmark, of which 1,431 Reichsmark was made during a total expected life span of nine months—6 RM per day minus 70 cents for food and clothes, times 30 (days) times 9 (months)—and another 200 Reichsmark was made after the prisoner's death, from his corpse, his clothing and valuable items he sometimes left behind (Fleischman, 71–73). According to Holocaust historian Raul Hilberg, life expectancy of a Jewish inmate at the I.G. Farben plant near Auschwitz was three to four months and at the outlying coal mines about one month (Hilberg, 996).

boss, *Reichsführer* Heinrich Himmler, instructed the *Einsatzgruppen* to regard all Jews as partisans and to shoot all male Jews of military age (Longerich, 198). From August, the *Einsatzgruppen* began to execute women, children and the elderly as well (Longerich, 207).

By then, Heydrich had already been instructed by *Reichsmarschall* Hermann Göring—whom Hitler had appointed as his first successor—to submit "*an overall plan of the preliminary organizational, practical and financial measures for the execution of the intended final solution* [Endlösung] *of the Jewish question*" (Arad, "Documents", 233).

Around the same time, *SS-Sturmbannführer* Rudolf Höss was ordered by Himmler to establish extermination facilities at the concentration camp where he was commander, Auschwitz.[18] Thus, after isolation, emigration and concentration, the final solution to the Jewish Question would be extermination.

---

18   At the Nuremberg trial after the war, Höss was questioned about this meeting with Himmler:

DR. KAUFFMANN: *Is it true that in 1941 you were ordered to Berlin to see Himmler? Please state briefly what was discussed.*

HOESS: *Yes. In the summer of 1941 I was summoned to Berlin to Reichsführer SS Himmler to receive personal orders. He told me something to the effect—I do not remember the exact words— that the Führer had given the order for a final solution of the Jewish question. We, the SS, must carry out that order. If it is not carried out now then the Jews will later on destroy the German people. He had chosen Auschwitz on account of its easy access by rail and also because the extensive site offered space for measures ensuring isolation.*" (qtd. in "Trial of the Major War Criminals", Vol. XI, 398).

Wannsee conference and the Final Solution

Hundreds of thousands of Jews had already been shot by the *Einsatzgruppen*, died of exhaustion from doing hard labor or from starvation or disease in the camps and ghettos, but mid-1941 the total annihilation of the Jews was made a primary goal for the first time. Because it would be highly counter-productive to the German war industry—which relied heavily on Jewish slave labor—there was some opposition from upper Nazi echelons against killing the Jews outright instead of simply working them to death, but the real decision had already been made.

On January 20, 1942, following up on Göring's order, Heydrich organized a conference for senior officials from several government ministries, in the Berlin suburb of Wannsee. For Heydrich, the main goals of the conference were to secure the cooperation of the various departments and to make sure that the implementation of the *Endlösung* would be regarded as an internal matter of the SS (Longerich, 310). A secondary goal was to determine who would be regarded as Jewish in the sense of the Final Solution and what to do with the *Mischlinge*.

In all, Heydrich invited fourteen people, among them officials from the Justice department, State department, Economics department and Ministry of the Interior, as well as representatives of administrations in charge of occupied territories in Eastern Europe.

Seven of the fifteen attendants (including Heydrich) held an SS rank, eight had earned a doctorate, six of which were in law.

The whole conference took no more than 90 minutes, after which Heydrich had secured the full cooperation of the various departments.

SS-Obersturmbannführer Adolf Eichmann was charged with the task of organizing the transports from all over German-occupied Europe to the six designated death camps, Auschwitz-Birkenau, Chelmno, Majdanek, Belzec, Sobibor and Treblinka.

The process of extermination — and its economy

Of these, Auschwitz was the most efficient. One reason for this was that Auschwitz Commandant Höss had made several improvements to the extermination process he had witnessed at Treblinka. For instance, instead of gas chambers capable of holding 200 people, like in Treblinka, he had gas chambers built that could hold 2,000 ("Trials of the Major War Criminals", Vol. XI, 417). For the gassing itself, Höss opted for Zyklon B, a crystallized prussic acid, instead of the monoxide gas used at Treblinka, because it worked faster ("Trials of the Major War Criminals", Vol. XI, 416). In his memoirs, Höss recalled:

"The gassing was carried out in the detention cells of Block 11. Protected by a gas mask, I watched the killing myself. In the crowded cells, death came

instantaneously the moment the Zyklon B was thrown in. A short, almost smothered cry, and it was all over... I must even admit that this gassing set my mind at rest, for the mass extermination of the Jews was to start soon, and at that time neither Eichmann nor I was certain as to how these mass killings were to be carried out. It would be by gas, but we did not know which gas and how it was to be used. Now we had the gas, and we had established a procedure."
(Hoss, 92–95).

Höss also went to great lengths to fool victims into thinking they were being deloused rather than gassed. Numbered coat hangers were put in the outer chamber for prisoners to hang their clothes on as they undressed. Meanwhile Jewish prisoners from the *Sonderkommando*—a special work detail forced to aid the SS with the extermination process—walked around, instructing victims to remember their coat hanger number so they could come back for their clothes after the delousing shower. The gas chamber itself was disguised as a shower room, with clean, whitewashed walls and shower heads hanging from the ceiling.

The gassing itself was handled by the SS, but the subsequent disposal and cleaning process was carried out by the prisoners of the *Sonderkommando*

(Greif, 2–6).[19] Selected on their arrival in the extermination camp and given the choice to join the *Sonderkommando* or die, most prisoners decided to join. Their living conditions were markedly better than those of regular camp prisoners. They had their own barracks, received better food and had access to liquor, cigarettes and medicines (Greif, 145, 234, 246, 374). They also did not have to fear to be killed at random like the other prisoners. In exchange, they did the dirty work.

After the gassing, the *Sonderkommando* removed the bodies from the gas chamber and brought them to a nearby room, where they were checked for valuables. Eyeglasses were lifted, rings slid of fingers, mouths checked for gold teeth, bridges and crowns, breaking them out if found (Greif, 321).[20] If a spot check by the SS revealed that gold had been missed, the prisoner responsible would be lucky to get away with a severe beating (Greif, 301).[21] Other body orifices were

---

19   Greif also describes how the *Sonderkommando* came into existence, evolving out of specific kommandos such as the *Krematoriums-Kommando* and the *Begrabungskommando* with the emergence of the policy to systematically exterminate all the Jews (Greif, 3–6).

20   Höss also mentions this in his testimony at Nuremberg ("Trial of the Major War Criminals", Vol. XI, 416).

21   Greif got this information from Leon Cohen, whose exclusive job in the *Sonderkommando* was to pull gold teeth from the gassed corpses. Cohen said that during his twelve-hour shifts new corpses would arrive every half-hour and each time he had ten minutes to pull out the gold teeth of some sixty to seventy-five corpses (Greif, 300–01).

checked as well for hidden valuables. After this, hair from female victims was shaved off. The teeth gold was melted into gold bars and transported to Berlin. The hair was sold to felt factories that used them in mattresses.

Meanwhile, prisoners from the *Kanada Kommando* collected the belongings from the gassed—suitcases, shoes, clothing, jewelry, photographs etc.—and brought them to a warehouse they called Canada (German: *Kanada*), a country that symbolized wealth in their eyes (Berg, 301). At the warehouse, everything was sorted and from there transported back to Germany at regular intervals.

Having checked the corpses, the *Sonderkommando* took the bodies to the crematorium, where they were put on metal stretchers and pushed into the furnace. In times of high volume, open-air pits were used together with the Crematoria. The remaining ashes were dumped in a lake nearby (Greif, 18, 95, 157, 251). While the corpses were incinerated, another detail of the *Sonderkommando* cleaned the gas chamber, washing away the blood, vomit, urine and excrement, and whitewashing the walls. Making everything ready for processing of the next group. Following this procedure 20,000 people could be disposed of within 24 hours at Auschwitz (Piper, 173–74). But that was at peak operation.

To prevent the inner workings of the extermination process to travel beyond the Crematoria, the SS replaced each *Sonderkommando* every four months or so. Of the thousands of prisoners active in one of the *Sonderkommandos* in Auschwitz-Birkenau between 1941–45, only about 80 lived to tell (Greif, 83). But even if none of them would have survived their story would have, as several of them wrote it down and buried it in the grounds of the Crematoria, right in the heart of darkness (Czech, 372). The documents were discovered years after the war.

Early 1942, when it became clear that Germany might not be able to hold on to all of its previously conquered territory in the East, on account of the failure of Operation Barbarossa (June-December 1941) and the subsequent Soviet counter-offensive, Heydrich met with *SS-Standartenführer* Paul Blobel to discuss the need to erase all traces of the mass executions (Arad, "Operation Reinhard", 170).

Heydrich was subsequently assassinated in Prague, before he could officially appoint Blobel, but not long after Gestapo chief *SS-Gruppenführer* Heinrich Müller put Blobel in charge of the secret operation, code-named *Sonderaktion 1005*, whose objective it was to cover up remaining evidence of the mass murders by exhuming all the bodies from mass graves and burn them (Arad, "Operation Reinhard", 170–71).[22]

---

22   Blobel had been the commanding officer of Sonderkommando

The *Sonderkommandos* charged with exhuming and burning the bodies were killed after their work was done.

On October 7, 1944, the Auschwitz *Sonderkommando* of Crematorium IV revolted after a rumor they would soon be 'transferred to another camp', SS-speak for extermination (Henry, 58). Before the revolt was suppressed, the *Sonderkommando* had succeeded in blowing up Crematorium IV, damaging it beyond repair. It was never used again. 250 *Sonderkommando* members lost their lives during the revolt, 200 others were shot by the SS as a reprisal and disposed of by the next *Sonderkommando* (Henry, 58). One month later, Himmler ordered the destruction of the remaining Crematoria.

On January 18, 1945, shortly before the Russians reached the camp, the SS marched the remaining 60,000 prisoners out of Auschwitz to Wodzislaw, 35 miles (56 km) away, from where they were put on freight trains to other camps (Rozett, 183). At least 15,000 of them died or were killed during this death march. Those who had been too weak or too sick to walk had been left behind at the camp. When the Russians liberated Auschwitz a few days later, on

---

4a of Einsatzgruppe C, which had, among other things, carried out the massacres at Babi Yar (in Kiev, Ukraine) on September 29–30, 1941. He was sentenced to death by the Nuremberg Tribunal and hanged in 1951.

January 27, about 7,000 of them were still alive (Stone, 41).

The figures

All told, approximately 6 million Jews were killed by the Nazis—about two thirds of the entire European Jewish population—4 million in extermination camps and another 2 million through mass shootings from the *Einsatzgruppen*, starvation, disease and exhaustion.[23] 3.3 million Soviet POWs also perished at the hands of the Germans, as did nearly 3 million non-Jewish Poles, between 220,000–1,500,000 Gypsies, 200,000 disabled, and between 3,000 and 10,000 homosexuals.[24]

---

23   At Nuremberg, the Austrian SS officer (and historian) Wilhelm Höttl testified about a conversation he had had with Adolf Eichmann, late August 1944, during which the latter had confided that, *"Approximately 4 million Jews had been killed in the various concentration camps, while an additional 2 million met death in other ways, the major part of which were shot by operational squads of the Security Police during the campaign against Russia."*(qtd. in "Trial of the Major War Criminals", Vol. III, 569).

24   In his *History of the Holocaust*, Jonathan Friedman notes that estimates about the number of Gypsies killed vary greatly, with the figure of 1.5 million at the high end, but the estimates he quotes in a subsequent note (44) are all around 200,000 (Friedman, 381, 384). The estimate of the number of mentally and physically disabled killed is more certain (Friedman, 138). On the number of homosexuals killed, Friedman notes that of the estimated 5,000–15,000 that ended up in concentration camps, two thirds died (395). The estimate on the number of non-Jewish Poles killed is from Kwiet and Matthaus (Kwiet, 258). Concerning the murder of Soviet POWs, Hannes Heer and Klaus Naumann write, in *War of Extermination: The German Military in World War II 1941–1944*: "*Between 22 June 1941 and the end of the*

An estimated 1.1 million Jews were exterminated in Auschwitz between September 1941-November 1944 (Gutman, 71).[25]

Auschwitz was also the only camp where prisoners were tattooed with a serial number—the ones who were given prisoner status that is—405,000 in total (Marrus, 1131). Of those, 261,000 died or were killed in Auschwitz. How many of the rest perished in other camps or died on death marches is unknown.

Working as a cashier at a mini-market in the heart of Jerusalem, Ms. Sagir says she is asked about the number on her forearm about ten times a day. One time, a police officer said "*God creates the forgetfulness so we can forget*", to which she responded "*Because of people like you who want to forget this, we will have it again.*"[26]

---

war, roughly 5.7 million members of the Red Army fell into German hands. In January 1945, 930,000 were still in German camps. A million at most had been released, most of whom were so-called "volunteers" (Hilfswillige) for (often compulsory) auxiliary service in the Wehrmacht. Another 500,000, as estimated by the Army High Command, had either fled or been liberated. The remaining 3,300,000 (57.5 percent of the total) had perished." (Heer, 80–81).

25   Gutman and Berenbaum note that this number is regarded as a minimum estimate.

26   Qtd. in Rudoren, "Proudly Bearing".

3

A BOMB

"My God, what have we done?"[1]

> Captain Robert Lewis, co-pilot of B-29 bomber
> Enola Gay, writing in the official log after dropping the
> atomic bomb 'Little Boy' on Hiroshima, August 6, 1945

ON SEPTEMBER 20, 2009, IRAN'S SUPREME LEADER, Ayatollah Ali Khamenei declared: *"We fundamentally reject nuclear weapons and prohibit the use and production of nuclear weapons."* (qtd. in Erdbrink, "Iran Denies"). When newly elected Iranian President Hassan Rouhani visited the U.N. General Assembly in New York four years later, he concurred that Iran would never *"seek weapons of mass destruction, including nuclear weapons."* (qtd. in Erdbrink, "Iran's Leaders").

Soothing words. Of course the main question in the West, including Israel—especially Israel—is whether they are true. Ever since an Iranian political opposition group in 2002 revealed that Iran had a nuclear program that included a uranium enrichment plant

---

1   Qtd. in MacPherson 2015.

in the vicinity of the city of Natanz and a heavy water production plant at the city of Arak, the developed world has stepped up its efforts to prevent Iran from ever getting the bomb.[2]

One of the main aims of the so-called P5+1 nations, the five permanent members of the U.N. Security Council—the United States, Russia, China, Britain and France—plus Germany, has been to prevent Iran from enriching uranium to the point where building a nuclear weapon would only be a matter of months. To that end, the P5+1 have followed a dual-track strategy since 2006, combining negotiations with U.N. Security Council resolutions demanding the country to halt uranium enrichment and imposing sanctions to force it to comply.[3-4] Incidentally (or perhaps rather

---

2   On August 14, 2002, Alireza Jafarzadeh, spokesman for the National Council of Resistance of Iran, presented new evidence about the existence of secret nuclear facilities in the cities of Natanz and Arak ("Iran and Nuclear Weapons").

3   A possible third track is the frustration of Iran's nuclear program through covert means, e.g., cyber warfare. An example is the computer worm Stuxnet, discovered in 2010, which was inserted in Iran's nuclear facility at Natanz and reportedly destroyed a fifth of Iran's nuclear centrifuges. It has been speculated (though not proven) that the worm was created by the United States and/or Israel.

4   United Nations Security Council Resolution 1696, adopted on July 31, 2006, demanded Iran suspend its uranium enrichment program "*or face possible economic, diplomatic sanctions*". After the country failed to do so, United Nations Security Council Resolution 1737 was passed on December 23 that same year, imposing the first sanctions. Between 2007–10, these sanctions were subsequently expanded through resolutions 1747, 1803 and 1929 ("Security Council Committee").

not incidentally), the P5 nations are also the first five nations that acquired the bomb for themselves.

Crucial discoveries and the British attempt to build the bomb

Britain was the first country to take a serious stab at building a nuclear bomb, in 1941. A few years earlier, on December 17, 1938, the German chemist Otto Hahn and his assistant Fritz Strassman had discovered nuclear fission of the heavy element uranium—i.e., the splitting of its nucleus—after bombarding it with neutrons, causing the release of a great amount of energy in the process.

A couple of months later, physicists Enrico Fermi, Leó Szilárd and Herbert Anderson proved that bombarding uranium with neutrons resulted in significant neutron multiplication, thus setting off a self-propagating chain reaction capable of releasing massive amounts of energy (Anderson, "Neutron Production"). They immediately realized their discovery could lead to the development of a nuclear bomb. Szilárd later said: "*that night* [March 3, 1939, after the definitive experiment] *there was very little doubt in my mind that the world was headed for grief.*" (qtd. in Rhodes, 292).

Initially, it was believed that several tons of uranium were needed to achieve the 'critical mass' necessary for a sustained nuclear chain reaction.[5] Though possible,

---

5   The German-Jewish physicist Rudolf Peierls, who had remained

it would hardly be practical. Still, the estimated destructive capability of a nuclear bomb would be so great that it prompted Szilárd to write a concerned letter to U.S. President Franklin Roosevelt on August 2, 1939, less than a month before Hitler invaded Poland. The letter was signed by Albert Einstein, who had readily agreed to lend his signature after Szilárd told him about the concept of sustained nuclear chain reaction and his experiment proving it. "*Daran habe ich gar nicht gedacht!*" ("I never even thought of that!") Einstein famously replied after Szilárd's explanation (qtd. in Rhodes, 305). In the letter to Roosevelt, Szilárd theorized that a nuclear bomb "*carried by boat and exploded in a port, might very well destroy the whole port together with some of the surrounding territory. However, such bombs might very well prove to be too heavy for transportation by air.*" (Einstein 1939).

But in March 1940, physicists Otto Frisch and Rudolf Peierls, both working at Birmingham University, calculated that only about one pound of pure uranium-235 (U-235) would be needed to produce a nuclear bomb with an explosive force equivalent to "*1,000 tons of dynamite*" (Frisch, "Memorandum"). They wrote a memo explaining the science that supported

---

in England after Hitler came to power in 1933, initially calculated that the needed critical mass was "*of the order of tons*" (qtd. in Rhodes, 321). The theoretical physicist Werner Heisenberg, who would be part of the German nuclear weapon project, believed it was about one ton (Bernstein, 129).

their conclusions and outlining the implications of their calculations—small bombs capable of massive destruction, large numbers of civilian casualties, including from nuclear radiation, and the urgency of getting the bomb before Germany.

It would later turn out that their calculations were incorrect (the minimum amount of U-235 needed for a sustained nuclear reaction is 115 pounds, not one) but the memorandum was a definite wake up call for the British, who soon established a committee, code-named M.A.U.D., to conduct a feasibility study on the production of a nuclear weapon (Rhodes, 340–41).

One year later, in the summer of 1941, as German tanks rolled into Russia during Operation Barbarossa, the M.A.U.D. committee reported that it would be possible to produce a nuclear bomb with a critical mass of about 25 lb (11,5 kg) of active material, that this bomb could be ready by the end of 1943 and that a plant capable of producing three such bombs per month would cost approximately 5 million pounds (M.A.U.D., "Report"). All of these statements would later prove incorrect, but the British war cabinet was sold. Churchill dryly commented: "*Although personally I am quite content with the existing explosives, I feel we must not stand in the path of improvement.*" (qtd. in Rhodes, 372).

One of the main reasons for the British effort was fear the Nazis would get the bomb. Germany had been at the vanguard of some early discoveries in the field of nuclear physics and had produced several prominent physicists, though a good deal of them had quit the country after 1933—many because they were Jewish—among them Albert Einstein, Leó Szilárd, Max Born, Otto Frisch, Rudolf Peierls, Lise Meitner, Edward Teller and Hans Bethe, to name a few.[6-7]

The British had also been alarmed by German efforts to produce greater quantities of heavy water at the Norwegian Hydrogen plant Norsk Hydro (Bernstein, 27). Heavy water, as had been recently discovered, could be used to produce plutonium, another element besides uranium capable of sustaining a nuclear chain reaction. German interest in heavy water therefore indicated they had made strong advances in nuclear research and might be attempting to produce enough fissile material for a bomb.

Later in the war it would become clear that around the same time the Americans decided to pull out all the stops in developing the bomb, the Nazis decided not to, chiefly because the scientists involved had

---

6   Enrico Fermi emigrated from Benito Mussolini's fascist Italy to the United States in the late 1930s, because of new Italian racial laws affecting his Jewish wife.

7   Several of the emigrated scientists had already made key discoveries in nuclear physics and would come to play an important role in the American effort to develop a nuclear bomb, the Manhattan Project. Who knows what would have happened if Hitler had been just a warmonger, instead of being equally hell-bent on the destruction of the Jews.

reported that the development of a nuclear weapon would take too long to make a difference in the war.[8-9]

Of course the British did not know exactly how far the Germans had progressed, and fear can be a powerful motivator. Therefore, aside from pouring resources into their own project, code-named *Tube Alloys*, they also sent Australian physicist and member of the M.A.U.D. Committee Dr. Mark Oliphant to the United States, to try and persuade the Americans to step up their efforts into nuclear weapons research. It worked, because in October 1941 President Roosevelt approved the atomic program, though it would be the Japanese attack on Pearl Harbor a few months

---

8   They were partially right, since Germany had indeed already been defeated by the time the Americans acquired the bomb. Then again, with the atomic bomb being such a game changer, any German military victory would have been rendered meaningless the moment one of its (still undefeated) enemies acquired it.

9   In *Hitler's Uranium Club: The Secret Recordings at Farm Hall*, Jeremy Bernstein publishes a fascinating discussion—held on August 6, 1945, just after the announcement that an atomic bomb had been dropped—between some of the most important German scientists who the Allies believed had worked on Nazi Germany's nuclear program (115–25). In an operation code-named 'Epsilon', meant to uncover how close Germany had come to a nuclear bomb, the scientists, who were detained by the Allies after the defeat of Germany, among them Otto Hahn and Werner Heisenberg, were interned at Farm Hall, a bugged house in Godmanchester, England. During the discussion, they express disbelief about the American success of developing and deploying a nuclear weapon and contemplate why the German effort was unsuccessful.

later that really ignited American enthusiasm for the project.[10]

Unlike the Germans, who were too impatient and had scared away one too many brilliant scientist, or the British, who were too optimistic about the cost, or the Russians, who were simply too busy fighting for their lives, the Americans had plenty of brilliant scientists (several of whom were coming from Germany), plenty of money, plenty of resources and a highly supportive government. Between 1942–45, the U.S. would spend a total of $1.9 billion on its nuclear program, known as the *Manhattan Project*, the equivalent of $25 billion in 2014 (Schwartz, 58).

The Manhattan Project

The Manhattan Project was a huge undertaking, employing some 130,000 people at its peak, the vast majority construction workers working on the various nuclear reactors (Jones, 344). But despite the magnitude of the workforce, very few people knew the full extent of what was actually going on. They erected accommodations, constructed roads, put up fences, pushed buttons, operated levers and watched meters, but they did not know what for.

---

10   After the war, Leó Szilárd said: "*If Congress knew the true history of the atomic energy project, I have no doubt but that it would create a special medal to be given to meddling foreigners for distinguished services, and Dr. Oliphant would be the first to receive one.*" (qtd. in Rhodes, 372).

One woman who worked in the laundry at the Monsanto Chemical Company, explained: "*The uniforms were first washed, then ironed, all new buttons sewed on and passed to me. I'd hold the uniform up to a special instrument and if I heard a clicking noise - I'd throw it back in to be done all over again. That's all I did - all day long.*" (qtd. in Atomic Energy Commission, "Script", 7).

Another, working at the Carbide and Carbon Chemical Company Plant, said: "*I stood in front of a panel board with a dial. When the hand moved from zero to 100 I would turn a valve. The hand would fall back to zero. I turn another valve and the hand would go back to 100. All day long. Watch a hand go from zero to 100 then turn a valve. It got so I was doing it in my sleep.*"(qtd. in Atomic Energy Commission, "Script", 8).

Some only found out years later they had worked at a place that had been part of the Manhattan Project, others never did. Of course there were also those, working at the project's principal laboratory in Los Alamos, New Mexico, who realized what they had been working on right after the Trinity Test, on July 16, 1945, when the first nuclear device was detonated at the Alamogordo Bombing and Gunnery Range (present-day White Sands Missile Range), some 200 miles from Los Alamos.

No more than a handful of people knew what was going on before that day, and even the few scientists present at the test didn't fully know what to expect. Would it work? Were they standing at a safe enough distance? What would it look like?

Before the test, Edward Teller, one of the theoretical physicists, had raised the possibility of the explosion igniting the atmosphere, which could perhaps cause a chain reaction eliminating all life on the planet (Rhodes, 418). Teller himself and fellow physicist Hans Bethe had subsequently calculated that such a self-propagating chain reaction was highly unlikely to occur, but did the calculation also prevent Teller from imagining—if only for a moment—a burning atmosphere consuming all in its path and ending life as we know it, as he was watching 'the gadget' (as it was called) fall from the bomb tower in Alamogordo? Indeed, did it prevent the others from thinking they might be at the verge of unleashing forces they still knew so little about? Especially since the evening before the explosion, Enrico Fermi, in an attempt to alleviate the nervous waiting, had offered to take bets from the other scientists on whether or not the bomb would ignite the atmosphere, and if so, whether it would destroy just New Mexico or the entire world (Rhodes, 664).

Fortunately, life as we know it was not eliminated, though the gadget did explode with a force equivalent to about 20,000 tons of TNT, big enough to completely evaporate the center of a city. There was a bright light that could be seen up to 180 miles away, a thundering shockwave traveling a 100 miles in each direction—even breaking a window 125 miles away—and a great mushroom cloud rising up 41,000 feet from the epi-center of the explosion (Groves, 1–2). Some called it beautiful.

Szilárd Petition and the decision to drop the bomb

Even before the Trinity Test Leó Szilárd had started circulating a petition among scientists working at the Manhattan Project, that sought to discourage President Harry S. Truman—who had succeeded to the presidency just a few months earlier, when Roosevelt died in office—from using the bomb against Japan. Szilárd suggested to first make public the terms of surrender to Japan and give the country a chance to lay down its arms, before resorting to the use of atomic bombs.

He also warned that using the bomb might "[open] *the door to an era of devastation on an unimaginable scale.*" (Szilard, "Petition"). And that, if "*rival powers*" would be permitted "*to be in uncontrolled possession of these new means of destruction, the cities of the United States as well as the cities of other nations will be in continuous danger of sudden annihilation.*".

The petition was signed by 69 other scientists but never made it through to the President.

An advisory scientific panel, consisting of Robert Oppenheimer, Enrico Fermi and others, found itself fundamentally divided as well, as became clear from its June 16 'Recommendations on the Immediate Use of Nuclear Weapons', with some favoring a *"military application best designed to induce surrender"*, and others proposing a *"purely technical demonstration"* (Cantelon, 47–48).

But there was still a war on and many in the government and the military saw the atom bomb as a quick way to end it, without further loss of American lives. No one knew for sure how many American soldiers would be killed in an all-out assault on an all-out resistant Japan, but it was clear the price would likely be very high, with official estimates running from 200,000 to as high as 4 million casualties.[11] On the other hand, key people in the government and the military also realized at this point that the surrender of Japan was only a matter of months, three to six at

---

11   Of course nobody could predict casualty rates with any certainty. All estimates looked at previous campaigns and tried to account for the likely level of participation from the Japanese civilian population. Thus, General Curtis LeMay arrived at 500,000 casualties, while a study by the Joint Chiefs of Staff estimated around 456,000 casualties — including 109,000 dead or missing — for the first part of the campaign, climbing to a total of 1,200,000 casualties of which 267,000 fatalities for the second part. Another study, done for the Secretary of War, estimated that conquering Japan in its entirety in case of large-scale participation by civilians could cost as much as 1.7-4 million American casualties.

the most. In other words, an invasion might not even be necessary.

Still, there were other reasons for wanting to actually use the bomb and drop it on a populated city instead of an uninhabited island somewhere in the Pacific. For one, a demonstration could go wrong. The prospect of telling the whole world about a $2 billion super bomb that had been worked on for three years, only to see it fail miserably at a test in front of the enemy (present and future ones) was not particularly alluring to military strategists. Dropping the bomb unannounced would give away far less in case of failure and insulate the U.S. from a potentially highly embarrassing incident.

And then there were the Russians, who everybody knew would be allies only for as long as the war lasted. Trying to wait out the Japanese would see a bigger piece of the Asian pie going to the Soviet Union, all the more so because the war in Europe had ended, freeing up Soviet forces to be redeployed in Asia. Also, in terms of containment, what better message could be sent to an overbearing, aggressive dictator like Joseph Stalin than dropping a nuclear weapon on an enemy city? Not only would it prove to him the U.S. really had the bomb, but also that it wasn't afraid to use it, thus effectively killing two birds with one atomic bomb.

So they dropped it.

Twice.

Hiroshima and Nagasaki figures

The uranium-based atomic bomb *Little Boy* was detonated over Hiroshima on August 6, 1945, at 08:15 local time, with a force equivalent to 16 kilotons of TNT, destroying 4.4 square miles. (Young, 42–61; McRaney, 4). Between 70,000–80,000 people were killed by the blast and subsequent firestorm, with an equal number of people injured (United States Government, "U.S. Strategic Bombing Survey", 16).[12] Three days later, on August 9, the plutonium-based atomic bomb *Fat Man* was detonated over Nagasaki, at 11:01 local time, with a force equivalent to 21 kilotons of TNT (Young, 42–61). An estimated 35,000–40,000 people died instantly, with about the same number of injured (United States Government, "U.S. Strategic Bombing

---

12   The survey acknowledges that accurate figures are impossible to give, since many people had already left because of declining activity in the cities, the constant threat of incendiary raids and government evacuation programs (United States Government, "U.S. Strategic Bombing Survey", 16).

Survey", 4).[13] The Empire of Japan surrendered six days later, on August 15.[14]

Nuclear arms race and MAD

As Leó Szilárd had predicted, the use of the A-bomb on Japan immediately triggered an international nuclear arms race. On August 29, 1949, only four years after Hiroshima and Nagasaki, the Russians conducted their own first successful nuclear weapons test, code-named *First Lightning*.

The Soviet atomic bomb project benefitted greatly from captured German facilities, resources, research and scientific personnel. The Russians also acquired valuable information from atomic spy Klaus Fuchs, a German-born physicist who had worked with Rudolf Peierls on the Tube Alloys project and under Hans Bethe at the Los Alamos Laboratory.[15]

---

13   In Hiroshima, a surging fire storm increased the devastation caused by the bomb, as did the flat terrain of the city. As the U.S. Strategic Bombing Survey states: "*In Nagasaki, no such fire storm arose, and the uneven terrain of the city confined the maximum intensity of the damage to the valley over which the bomb exploded. The area of nearly complete devastation was thus much smaller; only about 1.8 square miles.*" (United States Government, "U.S. Strategic Bombing Survey", 4).

14   The official Japanese instrument of surrender was signed on September 2, 1945.

15   Fuchs had fled Nazi Germany in 1933 because of his communist beliefs and was granted British citizenship in 1942. He gave the Soviets valuable information on the required atomic mass and the method of detonation, among other things (Trenear-Harvey, 78–79). Early 1950, Fuchs was arrested, tried and convicted to fourteen years imprisonment. After his release, he was allowed to emigrate to East Germany,

When the United States refused to share nuclear technology with the United Kingdom after the war—even though the U.K. had shared its knowledge with the U.S.—the British restarted their own nuclear program, successfully detonating their first atomic weapon on October 3, 1952, in the lagoon between the Montebello Islands, in Western Australia.

Realizing it had to join the atomic club if it wanted to remain a global power (and it most definitely did), France started a nuclear weapons program of its own in 1956. The French conducted their first successful test on February 13, 1960, in the Algerian Sahara desert.

China started a nuclear weapons program around the same time as France, but it took the Chinese a few years longer to get to their first successful test, on October 16, 1964. Since then, several other countries have joined the atomic club, India in 1974, Pakistan in 1998 and North Korea in 2006; Israel is also believed to possess nuclear weapons, although it has never publicly confirmed this.[16]

While the nuclear arsenals of Britain, France and China never exceeded the hundreds, the U.S. and the U.S.S.R went out of their way to achieve Mutually

---

where he continued his scientific career. He died in 1988, one year before the fall of the Berlin Wall.

16   Though these countries are known or believed to possess nuclear weapons, they are not recognized by the Non-Proliferation Treaty as 'nuclear-weapons states'. Only the first five are.

Assured Destruction (MAD) many times over, building up arsenals of tens of thousands of nuclear warheads, keeping strategic nuclear bombers in the air, nuclear submarines at sea and equipping underground missile silos with land-based intercontinental ballistic missiles (ICBMs), so nuclear retaliation was assured in any event.[17]

During the Cuban missile crisis of October 1962, all this aggressive-defensive posturing would bring both countries—and their allies—on the verge of assuring each other's destruction beyond the theoretical, but at the last moment saner heads prevailed.[18]

Since the 1980s, the two nuclear superpowers have worked together in reducing their gargantuan nuclear stockpiles. As of 2014, Russia still possesses an estimated 8,000 nuclear weapons though, while the U.S. is not far behind with some 7,300 nuclear weapons (Kristensen, 97).

---

17   As of 2014, the British nuclear weapons inventory counts an estimated 225 nuclear warheads, with a peak of some 500 in the 1970s (Kristensen, 97). For France, the total arsenal is estimated to be around 300, while China is believed to possess approximately 250 nuclear weapons, according to Hans Kristensen in "Worldwide deployments of nuclear weapons, 2014". Estimates of between 2,000–3,000 Chinese nuclear warheads have also surfaced, but these appear to be based on unsubstantiated rumors.

18   For the 1962 Cuban Missile Crisis, see *The Cuban Missile Crisis: How Close We Really Came to Nuclear War*.

Since they both still have so many, perhaps they could lease a couple to Iran on the condition it won't develop a nuclear weapon of its own.

Works cited

Allcorn, William. *The Maginot Line, 1928–45.* Oxford: Osprey Publishing. 2003. Print.

Anderson, Herbert L., Enrico Fermi, and Leo Szilard. "Neutron Production and Absorption in Uranium." *Physical Review.* Vol. 56. Aug. 1, 1939: 284–286. Print.

Arad, Yitzhak. *Belzec, Sobibor, Treblinka: The Operation Reinhard Death Camps.* Bloomington: Indiana UP. 1987. Print.

Arad, Yitzhak, Israel Gutman, and Abraham Margaliot, ed. *Documents on the Holocaust: Selected Sources on the Destruction of the Jews of Germany and Austria, Poland, and the Soviet Union.* Eighth edition. Lea Ben Dor, trans. U of Nebraska P. 1999. Print.

Atomic Energy Commission. "Script from a radio broadcast sponsored by Gulf Oil Corporation. The script includes live interviews with employees who lived and worked at Oak Ridge during the development of the atom bomb." Records of the Atomic Energy Commission, 1923–1978. Feb. 9, 1947. research.archives.gov/id/281583?q=281583. ARC: 281583. NAIL Control Number: NRCA-326-OAK004-RADSCRIP. Web. Aug. 25, 2015.

Bendersky, Joseph W. *A History of Nazi Germany: 1919–1945.* Rowman & Littlefield. 2000. Print.

Bernstein, Jeremy. *Hitler's Uranium Club: The Secret Recordings at Farm Hall.* New York: Copernicus. 2001. Print.

Billington, James H., and Library of Congress. *Respectfully Quoted: A Dictionary of Quotations*. Dover Publications. 2010. Print.

Boemeke, Manfred F., Gerald D. Feldman, and Elisabeth Glaser, ed. *The Treaty of Versailles: A reassessment after 75 Years*. Cambridge: Cambridge UP. 1998. Print.

Browning, Christopher R. *The Origins of the Final Solution: The Evolution of Nazi Jewish Policy, September 1939-March 1942*. U of Nebraska P. 2007. Print.

Cantelon, Philip L, Richard G. Hewlett, and Robert C. Williams, ed. *The American Atom: A Documentary History of Nuclear Policies from the Discovery of Fission to the Present."* Second Edition. U of Pennsylvania P. 1991. Print.

Chamberlain, Neville. "Peace for Our Time." Sep. 30, 1938. British Historical Documents. britannia.com. Web. Apr. 2, 2015.

Chamberlain, Neville. "Statement by the Prime Minister in the House of Commons on March 31, 1939." The Avalon Project: The British War Bluebook. avalon.law.yale.edu. n.d. Web. Apr. 2, 2015.

Chuĭkov, Vasiliĭ Ivanovich. *The Beginning of the Road*. Macgibbon & Kee. 1963. Print.

Churchill, Winston S. "The Few." Aug. 20, 1940. The Churchill Centre. winstonchurchill.org. Web. Apr. 3, 2015.

Churchill, Winston S. *Their Finest Hour*. Volume II of the Second World War. New York: Houghton Mifflin Harcourt. 1986. Print.

Churchill, Winston S. *Triumph and Tragedy: The Second World War, Volume 6*. RosettaBooks. 2010. First edition 1953. Print.

Churchill, Winston S. "We Shall Fight on the Beaches". June 4, 1940. The Churchill Centre. winstonchurchill. org. Web. Apr. 3, 2015.

Copeland, Jack, et al. *Colossus: The Secrets of Bletchley Park's Codebreaking Computers*. Oxford: Oxford UP. 2006. Print.

Craig, William. *Enemy at the Gates: The Battle for Stalingrad*. Old saybrook: Konecky & Konecky. 1973. Print.

Crew, David F. *Nazism and German Society, 1933–1945*. London: Routledge. 1994. Print.

Czech, Danuta. "The Auschwitz Prisoner Administration." In *Anatomy of the Auschwitz Death Camp*. Yisrael Gutman and Michael Berenbaum, ed. Bloomington: Indiana UP. 1994: 363–379. Print.

Dull, Paul S. *A Battle History of the Imperial Japanese Navy, 1941- 1945*. Annapolis: Naval Institute Press. 2013. Print.

Einstein, Albert, and Leo Szilard. "Einstein's Letter to Roosevelt." osti.gov. Aug. 2, 1939. Web. Aug. 24, 2015.

"Encyclopedia Judaica: Haavara." jewishvirtuallibrary.org. n.d. Web. Aug. 17, 2015.

Erdbrink, Thomas. "As Talks With U.S. Near, Iran Denies Nuclear Arms Effort." washingtonpost.com. Sep. 21, 2009. Web. Aug. 24, 2015.

Erdbrink, Thomas. "Iran's Leaders Signal Effort at New Thaw." *The New York Times*. Sept. 19, 2013. Print.

Fleischman, Richard K., Warwick Funnell, and Stephen P. Walker, ed. *Critical Histories of Accounting: Sinister Inscriptions in the Modern Era*. New York: Routledge. 2013. Print.

Fox, Margalit. "Rochus Misch, Bodyguard of Hitler, Dies at 96." *The New York Times*. nytimes.com Sept. 6, 2013. Web. Apr. 1, 2015.

Friedman, Jonathan C. *The Routledge History of the Holocaust*. Abingdon: Routledge. 2011. Print.

Frisch, Otto, and Rudolf Peierls. "The Frish-Peierls Memorandum." web.stanford.edu. n.d. Web. Aug. 25, 2015.

Fromkin, David. *A Peace to End All Peace: The Fall of the Ottoman Empire and the Creation of the Modern Middle East*. New York: Henry Holt. 2010. Print.

"German Jewish Refugees, 1933–1939." *Holocaust Encyclopedia*. United States Holocaust Memorial Museum. n.d. ushmm.org. Web. Aug. 14, 2015.

Gilbert, G.M. *Nuremberg Diary*. Da Capo Press. 1995. First Edition 1947. Print.

Glantz, David M. *Operation Barbarossa: Hitler's Invasion of Russia 1941*. The History Press. 2011. Print.

Greif, Gideon. *We Wept Without Tears: Testimonies of the Jewish Sonderkommando from Auschwitz*. Yale UP. 2005. Print.

Groves, L. R. "Memorandum For The Secretary of War, The Test." July 18, 1945. nsarchive.gwu.edu. Original source: U.S. National Archives. RG 77, MED Records, Top Secret Documents, File no. 4. Web. Aug. 26, 2015.

Guderian, Heinz. *Panzer Leader*. Da Capo Press. 2002. First published in New York in 1952. Print.

Gutman, Yisrael, and Michael Berenbaum, ed. *Anatomy of the Auschwitz Death Camp*. Bloomington: Indiana UP. 1998. Print.

Headland, Ronald. *Messages of Murder: A Study of the Reports of the Einsatzgruppen of the Security*

Police and the Security Service, 1941–1943. Cranbury: Associated UP. 1992. Print.

Heer, Hannes, and Klaus Naumann, ed. *War of Extermination: The German Military in World War II 1941–1944.* Berghahn. 2004. Print.

Henry, Patrick. *Jewish Resistance Against the Nazis.* Catholic U of America P. 2014. Print.

Hilberg, Raul. *The Destruction of the European Jews.* Volume III. Third Edition. Yale UP. 2003. Print.

Hitler, Adolf. *Mein Kampf.* John Chamberlain, ed. Reynal & Hitchcock. 1939. Print.

Holdstock, Douglas, and Frank Barnaby. *Hiroshima and Nagasaki: Retrospect and Prospect.* New York: Routledge. 2013. Print.

Hoss, Rudolf, Pery Broad, and Johann Kremer. *KL Auschwitz Seen by the SS.* Panstwowe Muzeum w Oswiecimiu. 1978. Print.

"Iran and Nuclear Weapons." c-span.org. Aug. 14, 2002. Web. Aug. 24, 2015.

Isom, Dallas Woodbury. *Midway Inquest: Why the Japanese Lost the Battle of Midway.* Bloomington: Indiana UP. 2007. Print.

Jones, Vincent C. *Manhattan, the Army and the Atomic Bomb.* Washington: Center of Military History, U.S. Army. 1985. Print.

Jukes, Geoffrey. *Hitler's Stalingrad Decisions.* Berkeley: U of California P. 1985. Print.

Kluckhohn, Frank L. "U.S. Declares War, Pacific Battle Widens." *The New York Times.* Dec. 8, 1941. Print.

Kristensen, Hans M., and Robert S. Norris. "Worldwide deployments of nuclear weapons, 2014." *Bulletin of the Atomic Scientists.* Vol. 70(5) 96–108. thebulletin. sagepub.com. Web. Aug. 27, 2015.

Kwiet, Konrad, and Jurgen Matthaus, ed. *Contemporary Responses to the Holocaust.* Westport: Praeger. 2004. Print.

Landau, Ronnie S. *The Nazi Holocaust.* New York: I.B. Tauris & Co. 2006. First edition 1992. Print.

Lichtblau, Eric. "The Holocaust Just Got More Shocking." *The New York Times.* Mar. 3, 2013. Print.

LIFE. "Defeat Ends In Surrender". Dec. 30, 1940. Web. Apr. 3, 2015.

Longerich, Peter. *Holocaust: The Nazi Persecution and Murder of the Jews.* Oxford: Oxford UP. 2010. Print.

MacPherson, Robert. "Seventy years on, few Americans regret Enola Gay's mission." news.yahoo.com. Aug. 4, 2015. Web. Aug. 24, 2015.

Marrus, Michael Robert, ed. *The Nazi Holocaust. Part 6: The Victims of the Holocaust, Volume 2.* Walter de Gruyter. 1989. Print.

M.A.U.D. Committee. "Report by M.A.U.D. Comittee on the Use of Uranium for a Bomb." London: Ministry of Aircraft Production. July 1941. fissilematerials.org. Web. Aug. 25, 2015.

McRaney, W, and J. McGahan. *Radiation Dose Reconstruction U.S. Occupation Forces in Hiroshima And Nagasaki, Japan, 1945–1946.* Washington: Defense Nuclear Agency. Aug. 6, 1980. Print.

Michman, Dan. *The Emergence of Jewish Ghettos during the Holocaust.* Cambridge: Cambridge UP. 2011. Print.

Miller, Donald L. *D-Days in the Pacific.* New York: Simon & Schuster. 2008. Print.

Misch, Rochus. *Hitler's Last Witness: The Memoirs of Hitler's Bodyguard*. Pen & Sword Books , trans. Frontline Books. 2014.

Molotov-Ribbentrop Pact. *Modern History Sourcebook: The Molotov-Ribbentrop Pact, 1939*. Web. Apr. 2, 2015.

New York Times. "Hitler is Pleased to Get Rid of Foes." *The New York Times*. Mar. 27, 1938. Print.

Nicosia, Francis R. *Jewish Life in Nazi Germany: Dilemmas and Responses*. Berghahn Books. 2010. Print.

Overy, Richard. *Russia's War: A History of the Soviet War Effort: 1941–1945*. New York: Penguin Group. 1998.

Pinkus, Oscar. *The War Aims and Strategies of Adolf Hitler*. Jefferson: McFarland & Company. 2005. Print.

Piper, Franciszek. "Gas Chambers and Crematoria." *Anatomy of the Auschwitz Death Camp*. Yisrael Gutman and Michael Berenbaum, ed. Bloomington: Indiana UP. 1994. 157–182. Print.

Pipes, Richard. *Communism: A History*. Modern Library Edition. New York: Random House. 2001. Print.

"Program of the National Socialist German Workers' Party." Avalon Project, Yale Law. n.p. n.d. avalon.law. yale.edu. Web. Aug. 13, 2015.

Rhodes, Richard. *The Making of the Atomic Bomb: 25th Anniversy Edition*. New York: Simon & Schuster. 2012. Print.

Richards, Denis. *The Royal Air Force 1939–1945 Vol. I: The Fight At Odds*. London: H.M. Stationery Office. 1953. Print.

Risser, Nicole Dombrowski. *France Under Fire: German Invasion, Civilian Flight, and Family Survival during World War II*. Cambridge: Cambridge UP. 2012.

Roberts, Geoffrey. *Stalin's Wars: From World War to Cold War, 1939–1953*. Yale UP. 2006. Print.

Roberts, Geoffrey. *Victory at Stalingrad: The Battle that Changed History*. Harlow: Pearson Education Limited. 2002. Print.

"Roll of Honour of "The Few"." *The Battle of Britain Historical Society*. battleofbritain1940.net. Web. Apr. 3, 2015.

Rozett, Robert, and Shmuel Spector. *Encyclopedia of the Holocaust*. Jerusalem Publishing House. 2000. Print.

Rudoren, Jodi. "Proudly Bearing Elders' Scars, Their Skin Says 'Never Forget'." *The New York Times*. nytimes.com. Sept. 30, 2012. Web. Aug. 13, 2015.

Schmuhl, Hans-Walter. *The Kaiser Wilhelm Institute for Anthropology, Human Heredity and Eugenics, 1927–1945:Crossing Boundaries*. Springer. 2008. Print.

Schnoor, Stefan, and Boris Klinge. "The last survivor of Hitler's downfall - The Fuhrer's bodyguard gives last interview." express.co.uk. May 15, 2011. Web. Apr. 1, 2015.

Schwartz, Stephen I, ed. *Atomic Audit: The Costs and Consequences of U.S. Nuclear Weapons Since 1940*. Washington: Brookings Institution. 1998. Print.

Sciolino, Elaine. "North of Paris, a Forest of History and Fantasy." *The New York Times*. nytimes.com. Nov. 2, 2008. Web. 3 Apr. 2015.

"Security Council Committee established pursuant to resolution 1737 (2006)." un.org. n.d. Web. Aug. 24, 2015.

Sherman, A. J. *Island Refuge: Britain and Refugees from the Third Reich 1933–1939*. Routledge. 2013. Print.

Stalin, Joseph. "Order No. 227 by the People's Commissar of Defence of the USSR". July 28, 1942. wikisource.org. Web. Apr. 4, 2015.

Steinweis, Alan E. *Studying the Jew: Scholarly Antisemitism in Nazi Germany*. Harvard UP. 2006. Print.

Steinweis, Alan E., and Robert D. Rachlin. *The Law in Nazi Germany: Ideology, Opportunism, and the Perversion of Justice*. Berghahn Books. 2013. Print.

Stone, Dan. *The Liberation of the Camps: The End of the Holocaust and Its Aftermath*. Yale UP. 2015. Print.

Szilard, Leo. "Petition to the President of the United States." July 17, 1945. trumanlibrary.org. Original source: U.S. National Archives, Record Group 77, Records of the Chief of Engineers, Manhatten Engineer District, Harrison-Bundy File, folder #76. Web. Aug. 26, 2015.

Trenear-Harvey, Glenmore S. *Historical Dictionary of Atomic Espionage*. Lanham: Rowman & Littlefield. 2011. Print.

Trial of the Major War Criminals before the International Military Tribunal. Nuremberg, 14 November 1945–1 October 1946. Nuremberg. 1947. loc.gov/rr/frd/Military_ Law/NT_major-war-criminals.html (gives access to all 42 volumes). Web. 2 Apr. 2015.

United States Government. *Peace and War: United States Foreign Policy, 1931–1941*. Dept. of State. Washington: United States Government Printing Office. 1943. Print.

United States Government. *U.S. Strategic Bombing Survey: The Effects of the Atomic Bombings of Hiroshima and Nagasaki, June 19, 1946*. War Department. Print.

"Versailles Treaty June 28, 1919." Avalon Project, Yale Law. Avalon. law.yale.edu. Web. July 23, 2015.

White, Matthew. *Atrocities: The 100 Deadliest Episodes in Human History*. New York: W.W. Norton & Company. 2012. Print.

Yahil, Leni. *The Holocaust: The Fate of European Jewry, 1932–1945*. Ina Friedman and Haya Galai, trans. Oxford: Oxford UP. 1990. Print.

Young, Robert W., and George D. Kerr. *Reassessment of the Atomic Bomb Radiation Dosimetry for Hiroshima and Nagasaki—Dosimetry System 2002*. Vol. 1. Hiroshima: Radiation Effects Research Foundation. 2005. Print.

Printed in Great Britain
by Amazon